a pocketful of RHYME
Imagination for a new generation

2006 Poetry Competition for 7-11 year-olds

YoungWriters

South West England Vol I
Edited by Michelle Afford

Young Writers

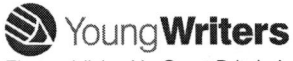

First published in Great Britain in 2006 by:
Young Writers
Remus House
Coltsfoot Drive
Peterborough
PE2 9JX
Telephone: 01733 890066
Website: www.youngwriters.co.uk

All Rights Reserved

© Copyright Contributors 2006

SB ISBN 1 84602 590 7

Foreword

Young Writers was established in 1991 and has been passionately devoted to the promotion of reading and writing in children and young adults ever since. The quest continues today. Young Writers remains as committed to the nurturing of poetic and literary talent as ever.

This year's Young Writers competition has proven as vibrant and dynamic as ever and we are delighted to present a showcase of the best poetry from across the UK and in some cases overseas. Each poem has been selected from a wealth of *A Pocketful Of Rhyme* entries before ultimately being published in this, our fourteenth primary school poetry series.

Once again, we have been supremely impressed by the overall quality of the entries we have received. The imagination, energy and creativity which has gone into each young writer's entry made choosing the poems a challenging and often difficult but ultimately hugely rewarding task - the general high standard of the work submitted ensured this opportunity to bring their poetry to a larger appreciative audience.

We sincerely hope you are pleased with this final collection and that you will enjoy *A Pocketful Of Rhyme South West England Vol I* for many years to come.

Contents

Calder House School, Colerne
Ayrton Fiorenzio (11)	1
Anthony Lane-Houston (11)	1
Lewis Hall (9)	2
Matthew Smith (8)	2
Nicole Nicholls (10)	3
Amelia Shale (8)	3
Henry Gallop (9)	4
Sam Billinghurst (7)	4
Jake Billinghurst (7)	5
Laurence Bunney (8)	5
Calum MacKnight White (9)	6
Isabelle La Turner (10)	6
Nathaniel Cooper (10)	7
Poppy Mills (10)	7
Anthony Duke (7)	8
Grace Hedge (10)	8
Max Totterman (8)	8

Darite Primary School, Liskeard
Alyce Martini-Richards (11)	9
Barrie-Jon Hutton (9)	9
Courtney Sexton (8)	10
Chloe Gunning (9)	10
Lianna Haywood (9)	11
Tilly Dimond (10)	11
Corrie McDonald (11)	12
Louise Sexton (11)	12
Rebecca Ferguson (10)	13
Holly Thorne (11)	13
Luca Martini (9)	14
Luke Serpell (10)	14
Bethany O'Shea (8)	15
Aaron Sexton (9)	15
Tristan Loughrey-Robinson (8)	16
Luke Payne (10)	16
Lauren Hedley (9)	17
Alex Sawley (10)	17
Rory Turnham (7)	18

Piers Loughrey-Robinson (10)   18
Archie Doidge (8)   19
Ryan Smith (7)   19
Andrew Brown (11)   20
Rosie Meitiner (11)   20
Leonard Bassett (8)   21
Natty Vine (10)   21
Aurellie Joy Relos (9)   22
Leeza Hodge (9)   23
Ben Ackland (9)   24
Gemma Wilkinson (8)   25
Beth Lewis (8)   26
Jacob Ferguson (8)   27
Sophie Tazzar (8)   28
Dylan Peel (11)   28
Sammy Vine (9)   29

Denbury Primary School, Newton Abbot
Ellie Doidge (10)   29
Abby Foster-Turner (10)   30
Ed Roberts (11)   30
Guy Bennett (10)   30
Hayley Wakefield (10)   31
Daniel Ponsford (10)   31
David Broughton (10)   31
Rebecca Kane (10)   32
Meah Howlett (10)   32
Timothy Mawson (10)   32
Tessa Burgin (10)   33
Harvey Woodfield (10)   33
Oliver Quant (10)   33
Jemima Richards (10)   34
Amy Pike & Paige Hammond (10)   34
Eleanor Hughes (10)   35
Lara Cosford (10)   35
Michael Bennett (10)   36
Michael Langler (11)   36

Ernesettle Community School, Plymouth
Lauren Goldsmith (10)   36
Zoe Clark (10)   37

Ben Ellis (10)	37
Mollie Neale (10)	37
Kieran Cadman (10)	38
Daniel May (10)	38
Kimberly Nathan (10)	39
Natalie Bone (10)	39
Shawnee Redding (10)	40
Harlie Uren (10)	40
Daniel Davies (10)	41
Kathryn Hammond (10)	41

Hannah More Primary School, Bristol

Lauren Jenkins (10)	42
Wadzani Mukambirwa (10)	43
Seanique Reuben (9)	44
Layla Henry Smith (10)	45
Emily Richer (10)	46
Declan Batt (10)	47
Alyssa Small (9)	48
Dean Eatwell (10)	48
Daniel Millin (10)	49

Nailsworth CE Primary School, Nailsworth

George Mole (10)	49
Jade Lefeuvre (10)	50
Jack Newman (9)	50
Sara Tasnim (10)	51
Jasmine Rosser (10)	51
Luke Daniels (10)	52
Megan Farrer (10)	53
Jacob Elliot Harris (10)	54
Henrietta Ruby Davis (10)	55
Jack Sessions (10)	56
Declan Scott (10)	57
Milly Griffin (10)	58
Marcus Shortland (10)	59
Ben Wear (10)	60
Eleanor Kate Milner (10)	61
Harry Dowdeswell (9)	62
Callum Gainey (10)	62

Jason Jones (10) — 63
Terri Ann Smith-Gardiner (9) — 63

Rushall CE Primary School, Pewsey
Gemma Mansell (9) — 64
Bethany Smith (10) — 64
Alice Spanswick (10) — 65
Dominic Tandy (10) — 65
Sam Flippance (8) — 66
Jamie Russell (10) — 67
Chloe Beaven (10) — 68
Laura Tyley (11) — 68
Zoe Spanswick (11) — 69
Jacob Garrett (9) — 69
Kristan Menard (11) — 70

St Mary's CE (VA) Primary School, Portbury
Gemma Ogden (9) — 70
Peter Kearsley (8) — 71
Thomas Scanlan (9) — 71
Eleanor Grey (9) — 72
Kira Phillipou (7) — 72
Dan Steven (9) — 73
Alice Robinson (9) — 73
Abbie Cooper (9) — 74
Molly Cheek (7) — 74
Georgia Weekes (9) — 75
Ben Collins (9) — 75
Rob Lange (9) — 76
Georgia Ross (9) — 76
Jack Edwards (9) — 76
Emma Adamson (9) — 77
Esme Pain (7) — 77
Megan Stephens (8) — 77
Adam Grey (10) — 78
Georgia Oliver (7) — 78
Emily Cosway (10) — 78
Paige Robinson (11) — 79
Alex Smith (10) — 79
Jake Wherlock (8) — 79
Emily O'Hara (10) — 80

Thomas Ryan (11) — 80
Leah Collins (10) — 80
Georgia Phillipou (11) — 81
Bethany Hawker (11) — 81
Alex Phillipou (10) — 82
Polly Snell (11) — 82
Amelia Landon (11) — 83

St Michael's Junior School, Twerton
Luke Jones (9) — 83
Sydney Grizzell (9) — 83
Alicia Magner (9) — 84
Thomas Smith (9) — 84
Sophia Bevan (9) — 84
Callum Harding (9) — 84
Matteo Weeks (9) — 85

St Thomas More Catholic Primary School, Cheltenham
Syd Haskayne (10) — 85
Stephen Lumbard (8) — 85
Megan Jones (9) — 86
Rudi Polster (9) — 86
Emily Domm (9) — 86
Madaleine Chambers (8) — 87
Phoebe Middlecote (9) — 87
Beth Garthwaite (9) — 87
Charlie Mustoe (9) — 88
Poppy Wall (9) — 88
Kerry Davis (9) — 88
Kirsty Simons (9) — 88
Ellie Garthwaite (9) — 89

Westbury-on-Severn CE Primary School, Westbury-on-Severn
Sam Batham (9) — 89
Matthew Ridler (11) — 89
Eleanor Burrows (10) — 90
Darcey Lowe (10) — 90
Elena Morris (10) — 91
Matthew Golledge (10) — 91
Jack Mantle (10) — 92

Joe Williams (11)	92
Emily Packman (11)	93
Rebecca Smith (9)	93
Georgia Gibson (10)	94
Tom Williams (9)	94
Michael Stalker (9)	95
Sophie Jackson (9)	95
Bethan Ridler (9)	96

Widey Court Primary School, Plymouth

Holly Olinda Wyatt (9)	96
Caitlin Gerry (9)	97
Chanelle Williams (9)	97
Rebecca Palmer (11)	98
Savannah Hicks (9)	98
Laura Whitemore (8)	98
Abigail Stoneman (9)	99
Matthew McDonald (8)	99
Courtney Hackett (9)	99
Emily Wooltorton (10)	100
Tess Lyddon (10)	100
Charlotte Floyd (11)	101
Sarah Horswell (10)	101
Ashley Hutchings (9)	101
Emily Carter (11)	102
Joe Balsdon (8)	102
Holly Owens (11)	103
Danielle Wills (9)	103
Jade Hawkings (9)	104
Hannah Ford (9)	104
Jordan Moore (11)	105
Chloe Blackmore (10)	105
Ryan Hateley (9)	106
Sacha Mills (11)	107
Anna Chow (11)	108

The Poems

Going To School

I ran and ran
But the bullies were too fast,
They caught me.
They took my lunch box,
They kicked it in the river,
They beat me with names,
They left me on my hands and knees.
I heard them laughing in the distance.
I never want to go to school again.

They are big now, so am I.
I've got lots of friends,
Now they have none.
I could get my own back
But the memories of pain
Won't let me.

Ayrton Fiorenzio (11)
Calder House School, Colerne

Trenches

Bullets, bullets, bullets
Tearing through gas.
A man fell, fell in the jaws of death,
Bullets, bullets, bullets.

Gas bombs dropped,
'Run, run!' shouted the general!
Bombs to the right of them,
Bombs to the left of them.

Finally it quietened down,
Quietened down, quietened down,
As sleep took him.

Anthony Lane-Houston (11)
Calder House School, Colerne

The Giant JCB

It pulls out its hard, scratched hand,
Lifting its heavy load.
Its head spins round
And the eyes flash wide open.

Air flows to the long arm
And the elbow moves
To empty the sandy shovel,
Vibrations from the pumping heart
Make rust and dust fall and flutter.

The heavy feet of the marauding monster
Climb up the hill,
Unloading its heavy load.
It clunks and clanks and starts digging.

At the end of the day
Its eyes close
And the digger waits . . .
Until the next time.

Lewis Hall (9)
Calder House School, Colerne

Happiness

Happiness is
A kiss and a hug,
Having a birthday,
Making new friends.

Happiness is
Love all around me,
Watching a sunset,
Getting a pet.

Happiness is
Going to the park,
Playing with my mum,
And my dad smiling at me.

Matthew Smith (8)
Calder House School, Colerne

The Sea

Suddenly the sea
Sways and swishes from side to side
It will not stop at all,
It sprays and sprays from side to side.

On the tumbling, rumbling rocks
Were many sea creatures.
Octopuses, sea snakes just lying there.
Crashing against the rocks and sand
Were many shells,
Broken by the rough waves.
Many fish of different colours
Were darting through the water.

From the cliffs you see
A beautiful sight,
Waves crashing as
The rocks came tumbling down.

As night falls
The sea gently calms,
All is quiet, not a sound,
And the sea creatures sleep.

Nicole Nicholls (10)
Calder House School, Colerne

Mummy

Mummy is
A beautiful butterfly,
The scent of a rose,
A soft woollen cardigan.

Mummy is
A kiss and a hug,
A big happy smile,
A delicious meal,
Mummy is special.

Amelia Shale (8)
Calder House School, Colerne

The Sea

The sea came smoothly in
On a sunny summer morning.
Over the shells the sea flowed
And the seaweed washed up the beach.

The sea showed some shining shells
As one by one the ships
Softly went out to sea.
Sometimes you can see
Fish glide through the water.

As the waves flowed out
To the deeper water
Seaweed was left on the beach
And the ships would return for the night.

Henry Gallop (9)
Calder House School, Colerne

Happiness

Happiness is

Watching a sunset,
A newborn puppy,
Or going on holiday.

Happiness is
Gliding down a waterslide,
Playing with dogs
And getting a new pet.

Sam Billinghurst (7)
Calder House School, Colerne

Happiness

Happiness is
Watching a sunset on a hill,
Going on holiday,
Visiting my cousins.

Happiness is
A newborn baby,
Cycling with my dad
And a fluffy white rabbit.

Happiness is
Playing with my dog,
Having lots of friends
And warm soft cuddles.

Jake Billinghurst (7)
Calder House School, Colerne

Anger

Anger is
When I have no friends
Punching and kicking
Hot, boiling lava.

Anger is
Fighting with light sabres
Waging a war
Bullying others.

Laurence Bunney (8)
Calder House School, Colerne

Poseidon

The sea is an angry god,
He is Poseidon,
God of the sea,
Angry as can be.
He is wrecking ships
With his waves
He blows boats passing by,
Throwing his trident at the sea,
Making waves shatter the surface of the sea.

But when the sea is calm
Poseidon is resting.

Calum MacKnight White (9)
Calder House School, Colerne

Blue

Blue is as beautiful
As the song of a robin on a winter's day.
Blue is as delicate as a snowflake,
As clear as glass,
As soft as a feather,
As fresh as water.
It smells like a blackberry pie
Fresh from the oven,
As calm as a summer's sea
That's what blue's like to me.

Isabelle La Turner (10)
Calder House School, Colerne

Mummy

Mummy is
A soft, warm jumper,
A bright red tulip,
Chocolate chip cookies
Melting in your mouth.

Mummy is
A big, wide smile,
A goodnight hug,
A listening ear,
My mummy is precious.

Nathaniel Cooper (10)
Calder House School, Colerne

Daddy

Daddy is
A comfy armchair
A cuddle at night
A happy smile.

Daddy is
A jacket potato
A walk with Bradley
A special hug
Daddy is the greatest!

Poppy Mills (10)
Calder House School, Colerne

Happiness

Happiness is
When the horses are sold,
A new dog,
Or when Mummy's got time
To play with me.

Happiness is
When my dog jumps up
And says hello,
Water running down my face
Or if I win a medal!

Anthony Duke (7)
Calder House School, Colerne

Snow

She comes in winter,
She makes my house and garden
All white.
She touches everything
With her long white nails.
As her silken dress floats on the ground
Everything turns white.
Can you think of her favourite colour?

Grace Hedge (10)
Calder House School, Colerne

The Sea

The sea shimmers and sparkles in the scorching sun.
Spectacular sandcastles stand on the shore.

The wild wind whisks up the waves,
Fish float furiously at the water's edge.

Wild waves crash upon the sea
Shining in the light of the midnight moon.

Max Totterman (8)
Calder House School, Colerne

The Golden Eagle

There you flutter,
In search of prey,
Suddenly something is spotted,
A small bird.
You shoot down,
As fast as a bullet,
Wings wide
And long like a motorway,
Treeless areas you prefer.

No animals hunt you,
But you hunt them.
Humans are your only fear,
You build your nest,
High up,
So no humans are in reach.
When your young are hungry,
They make a *yip yip* sound,
Like a ringing doorbell.
The golden eagle is the king of the sky.

Alyce Martini-Richards (11)
Darite Primary School, Liskeard

The Penguin

The penguin is a torpedo underwater,
Waddling instead of walking,
Big yellow feet,
A black body,
With a white centre,
Alert and deadly,
It dives into the water,
Snap!
A fish is devoured,
The penguin is the king of the ice.

Barrie-Jon Hutton (9)
Darite Primary School, Liskeard

The Magic Box
(Based on 'Magic Box' by Kit Wright)

I will put in my box . . .
The smooth, soft cats miaowing stroking their fur on a hot
summer's day.

I will put in my box . . .
The bark of a wild dog racing around in the night.

I will put in my box . . .
The smell of the pasta Bolognese
And the smell on a dark starry night.

I will put in my box . . .
The feel of gooey chocolate icing all around the cake.

My box is fashioned from bits of blue wedding dresses
And giant shark eyelashes.

In my box . . .
I will ride on a dolphin on a lovely sunny beach.
I will play with my friends and we will see the dolphins
And we will taste the salty water once again.

Courtney Sexton (8)
Darite Primary School, Liskeard

The Jellyfish

There you float,
Drifting through the sea,
Glowing in the dark,
Ready to catch fish.
Moving slowly and steadily,
Venom spits out of your tentacles,
Your soft, sly body slithers like a snake,
Through the water.
Pounce! You wrap your tentacles round your food.
Dead!
The jellyfish is the queen of the ocean.

Chloe Gunning (9)
Darite Primary School, Liskeard

The Magic Box
(Based on 'Magic Box' by Kit Wright)

I will put in my box . . .
A bang of flaming fireworks on a dark and windy night,
The loveliest taste of a smooth but hard ice cream on a summer's day.

I will put in my box . . .
A freshly baked carrot cake on a cold and windy night,
The brightest sunset in the light sky on a calm and cold evening.

My box is hand-blown by an ancient angel from high Heaven.
Its corners are built of stems from a fluffy flower.
Its hinges are created of shining white teeth from a snappy shark.

I shall sing in my box.
I will be a superstar singing on TV.
I will sing all day and through the night.
I shall sing with a real star glistening in the bright bold beam of light.

Lianna Haywood (9)
Darite Primary School, Liskeard

The Elephant

The elephant . . .
A humble animal,
A gentle giant,
Wrinkly and rough like leather boots,
Skin the colour of thundery rain clouds.
Stumbling along,
Shaking the ground,
Animals running away,
As if they are being chased.
It scoops up the leaves,
Its trunk a spoon,
So peaceful,
The elephant, the king of mammals.

Tilly Dimond (10)
Darite Primary School, Liskeard

The Green Anaconda

The green anaconda is . . .
A magnificent creature.
Appears scaly and as rough as sandpaper,
But really as smooth as silk.
A combination of mixed green,
Brown patches,
Makes it camouflage in its surroundings.
Other animals, cautious,
Approaching the water's edge.
Waiting to pounce on its meal like a lion,
Moving . . . focussed . . . ready,
Splash!
Powerful jaws clench its prey.
The green anaconda . . .
Is the king of all swamps.

Corrie McDonald (11)
Darite Primary School, Liskeard

The Snow Tiger

The snow tiger is . . .
A giant snowball,
With pointy, sharp teeth,
Watching prey,
From a great distance.
Pouncing like a shark attacking,
Its heart beats,
Like a drum,
Boom, boom, boom.
Roaring like,
Rumbling thunder,
The snow tiger is the ruler of the snow.

Louise Sexton (11)
Darite Primary School, Liskeard

The Tree Frog

There he sits,
Eyes closed,
Asleep.
Eyes open suddenly,
Like the shutter of a camera,
Glaring, left, right, left, right.
Skin like a sunset,
Legs so powerful and able,
Croaking hard,
Waiting . . .
For tasty insects.
The enemy is squirted with poisonous juice,
He is the king of the croakers.

Rebecca Ferguson (10)
Darite Primary School, Liskeard

The Octopus

The octopus is . . .
A multicoloured rainbow,
Eyesight like a hawk,
Gliding swiftly but silently,
Along the sandy seabed.
Food comes into sight,
Tentacles shoot out . . .
Attack!
Like a cheetah pouncing,
The enemy approaches
Squirt!
Black ink everywhere,
Day has turned into night.
The octopus is the ruler of the sea.

Holly Thorne (11)
Darite Primary School, Liskeard

The Magic Box
(Based on 'Magic Box' by Kit Wright)

I will put in my box . . .
The sweet smell of a delicate raspberry
On a summer's day.

I will put in my box . . .
A touch of a silky Arsenal shirt fresh
From a buzzing washing machine.

I will put in my box . . .
The taste of a fresh pineapple
Just cut and covered with melted chocolate.

I will put in my box . . .
The sight of a young dolphin
Diving in a fresh, calm blue sea with other dolphins.

I'd go surfing in the scorching sea off the USA.
I'd play football in the green stadium of Arsenal FC,
And ice hockey in the freezing stadium and score.
I'd go to Italy for a peaceful holiday.

My box is carved with shiny sparkling diamonds.
Gold bent swords poke from its dusty old top.
Freezing, shiny icicles melt on the box
And stuck on the top, a blood-coloured ruby stiff as a rock.

Luca Martini (9)
Darite Primary School, Liskeard

The Great White

The shark turns like a blade,
It's as quick as a lightning bolt,
He slashes through meat like a bullet,
Eyes turn as quick as a blink.

Grey as lead,
With 3,000 teeth like razors,
As big as a house,
The shark is the king of the sea.

Luke Serpell (10)
Darite Primary School, Liskeard

My Magic Box
(Based on 'Magic Box' by Kit Wright)

I will put in my box . . .
The splashing of people's colourful shoes on a rainy morning.

I will put in my box . . .
The gorgeous taste of fresh, ripe strawberries on a summer's day.

I will put in my box . . .
The beautiful smell of my mum's new perfume on a Christmas
                                                            morning.

I will put in my box . . .
The warm fur of my little hamster on a cold morning.

I will put in my box . . .
The young birds flying high in a clear blue sky on the first day
                                                            of spring.

My box is built up with golden eggs and its hinges are pure white
Like angels' wings.
It has a circle of glass in the middle blown by a goddess.

In my box I will go to the theatre in the busy town of London
And meet famous ballet dancers.
Then dance with them in front of celebrities in a tutu the colour of
A pristine pink petal.

Bethany O'Shea (8)
Darite Primary School, Liskeard

The Kangaroo

The kangaroo has . . .
Eyes like a two-pound coin,
A pouch like a plastic bag,
A powerful bite to protect,
Claws that scratch like daggers,
The kick of a horse,
Is a vegetarian,
It grinds its food like a hammer,
The kangaroo is the king of Australia.

Aaron Sexton (9)
Darite Primary School, Liskeard

The Magic Box
(Based on 'Magic Box' by Kit Wright)

I will put in my box . . .
The kaboom of a drum being banged by a stick in an ancient forest,
The swish of a slippery swing on a silent night.

I will put in my box . . .
A shock of shocking lightning on a stormy day,
The screeching pen on a dull whiteboard in a dusty classroom.

I will put in my box . . .
The delicious smell of carrot cake made from carrot on a winter's day,
The lovely smell of chocolate cake being baked in the kitchen.

I will put in my box . . .
The young taste of chewy marshmallows cooked in the oven.

My box is made from molten magma.
The hinges are made of the finger joints of a dragon
And its claws are locks to keep in the secrets.

In my box
I would climb a cliff and reach a peak and climb the next mountain.

Tristan Loughrey-Robinson (8)
Darite Primary School, Liskeard

The Racoon

A creature with black and white stripes,
Claws sharp as knives,
Teeth pointed like a dagger,
A masked face like a secret agent.
Loud noises outside,
Bang, bang, crash, crash!
Falling bins, bags ripping,
Sweeping a backyard,
Like a stormy ocean.
The racoon truly is the lord
Of all scavengers.

Luke Payne (10)
Darite Primary School, Liskeard

The Magic Box
(Based on 'Magic Box' by Kit Wright)

I will put in my box . . .
The wild roar of the crashing waves on a thundery night,
The constant splattering of hail on a snowy night.

I will put in my box . . .
The lovely taste of a fudge cake on a summer evening,
The beautiful smell of a flower's nectar on a spring morning.

I will put in my box . . .
The gorgeous sunset on an autumn day,
The soft touch of a hamster's fur on a winter morning.

My box is fashioned with gold beads and ice as hinges.
It has tissue stars on the inside and a piece of wedding dress
                                                on the other side.
It has roses carved on the sides.
As a final touch, a piece of love all over it.

I will play with my friends in my box,
We will play hide-and-seek, I spy and up and down.
When I go to sleep the light will go black and my box will close
                                                on the ocean waves.

Lauren Hedley (9)
Darite Primary School, Liskeard

The Chameleon

Slow and steady like a caterpillar,
An acrobat,
Agile as a monkey,
Silent.
Colours changing like a disco ball,
Its tongue a bullet,
And its mouth is the gun.
Its eyes are the cameras, searching . . .
The chameleon is the agent of the jungle.

Alex Sawley (10)
Darite Primary School, Liskeard

The Magic Box
(Based on 'Magic Box' by Kit Wright)

I will put in my box . . .
The wonderful taste of fresh, slimy spaghetti served by an Italian
waiter.

I will put in my box . . .
The smell of carrot cake cooking carefully in the oven.

I will put in my box . . .
A motorbike roaring and revving fast,
Scalding hot lava just shooting out high from the crater.

I will put in my box . . .
The touch of a silky spider climbing up my arm.

My box is soft with tiger's fur which is the darkest orange ever.
The hinges are pike's clasps.

In my box
I will ride away on my motorbike, revving across the land at a speed
Faster than a jaguar.

Rory Turnham (7)
Darite Primary School, Liskeard

The Komodo Dragon

There you crouch,
A stealthy hunter stalking its prey,
A roaring crowd,
Like angry lions fighting in a pride,
A fire-breathing dragon,
Hunting down a satisfying meal,
A long, slim creature,
Green scaly skin,
Jagged spikes along its back and tail,
The Komodo dragon is a mythical beast . . .
Returned.

Piers Loughrey-Robinson (10)
Darite Primary School, Liskeard

The Magic Box
(Based on 'Magic Box' by Kit Wright)

I will put in my box . . .
A cluck of a clever chicken on a smelly farm,
The *zooming zip* of a big bullet in a war zone.

I will put in my box . . .
The sweet taste of mushy marshmallows on Bonfire Night.,
The spicy taste of a hot vindaloo on a scorching summer day.

I will put in my box . . .
The smell of ponging petrol leaking from a car on a misty morning,
The tears of a gigantic giant on a sultry seashore.

I will put in my box . . .
The sight of Gavin Henson on a sunny day,
The sight of a gigantic Roman coliseum.

My box is created from shiny brass bullets.
It's encrusted with silver, smooth grenade pins, hinged with ammo
belts.

I shall play rugby and meet Gavin Henson and return home battered
and bruised.

Archie Doidge (8)
Darite Primary School, Liskeard

The Magic Box
(Based on 'Magic Box' by Kit Wright)

I will put in my box . . .
Eating spicy curry on a warm misty night with my brother.

I will put in my box . . .
Bonfire Night with exploding rockets on a crisp, cold night,
Sailing high into the sky.
Touching my trumpet with my strong fingertips.

My box is made from golden steel, motorbike springs and a
silvery lock.

Ryan Smith (7)
Darite Primary School, Liskeard

The Wolf

The wolf is . . .
A ferocious grey cloud in the snow,
Which prowls after helpless elk.
The time is right . . . it darts,
Pierces the tender neck,
Drawing blood.
Agonising pain,
The kill is made,
Howls erupt from the killer,
The noise is deafening.
Yellow, bloodshot eyes are hidden,
Grey eyelids in their place,
Then evilness returns to slice meat,
Satisfied hunger.
The wolf is the king of the snowy forest.

Andrew Brown (11)
Darite Primary School, Liskeard

The Polar Bear

The polar bear is . . .
An unnoticed white splodge in a painting,
Its fur white like snow,
Soft as a purring Persian cat,
Its nose a black button.
Hunting silently like the air,
Leaping into icy water,
Clawing its fish,
Magnificent muscles,
Tear its tough food.
Protective parent,
Defends its cubs by charging,
Its hind legs flex as the wolf approaches,
Teeth appear and it growls,
Frightens its predator away,
The polar bear is the ruler of the ice.

Rosie Meitiner (11)
Darite Primary School, Liskeard

My Magic Box
(Based on 'Magic Box' by Kit Wright)

I will put in my box . . .
The smell of chocolate cake cooling, ready to be eaten.

I will put in my box . . .
A wobbly jelly to be cut in half and eaten.

I will put in my box . . .
A rabbit to be fed on a sunny day.

I will put in my box . . .
A pizza cut up with a sweet lime and pineapple on the top.

I will put in my box . . .
A cool strawberry ice cream and sweet red cream.

I will put in my box . . .
Fish and chips and cola.

Leonard Bassett (8)
Darite Primary School, Liskeard

The Lion

The lion has . . .
A belly like a melon,
Teeth like sharp knives, white as silk,
Eyes like pound coins.
A tail like a whip,
Whiskers like pipe cleaners,
A mane, spread like the sun.
Its ears like a number six,
Hidden behind his golden mane.
His body as stiff as a log,
Before hunting like a cheetah.
Paws like large drums,
A roar like a train.
The lion is the king of the jungle.

Natty Vine (10)
Darite Primary School, Liskeard

My Magic Box
(Based on 'Magic Box' by Kit Wright)

I will put in my box . . .
The creak of the dusty, decorated door in the creepy castle,
The scary sound of the crashing car in the dark, gloomy night.

I will put in my box . . .
The miaow of the crazy, colourful cat in the noisy night,
The boom and the glamorous gun in the cowboy's shirt.

I will put in my box . . .
The smell of a dusty door on a snowy day,
The taste of a crunchy chocolate biscuit in the winter night.

I will put in my box . . .
The sight of a sun-shape in the sunset,
The soft sand on a beautiful beach.

My box is designed like a fairy's wing, twinkling, glittering like a star in the night.
It is encrusted with crystal and sparkling diamonds.
Its corners are the jawbone of a dangerous tiger.

I shall travel in my box
In the cold water on the seashore at the beach in the round sunshine
At the bottom of a huge hill.

Aurellie Joy Relos (9)
Darite Primary School, Liskeard

My Magic Box
(Based on 'Magic Box' by Kit Wright)

I will put in my box . . .
The soft fur of an exquisite rabbit on a rainy day,
Cold fresh air in the beautiful countryside on a gloomy Friday,
The ticking of a copper clock in a warm kitchen.

I will put in my box . . .
The swish of a rusty swing in a playful park,
Spicy vindaloo on a sunny summer Sunday,
Lashing lighting on a November night,
The zip of a speeding zipwire in an exciting park,
A bright coloured honeybee buzzing in a lush green meadow,
A sparkling sea shimmering in the blazing sunset.

I will put in my box . . .
The crackly cry of a chicken finding corn in a barn,
The rattle of rushing rain on a jungle's canopy,
A groan of a great storm on a thatched house.

My box is fashioned from fairy wings and furry angel wings.
It's encrusted with exquisite emeralds and bright blue beautiful
                                                    sapphires.
Its corners are the jaw joints of a chicken.

I will read in my box,
The Harry Potter book series,
Then lie down on a sun-coloured beach and after, bathe in a
                                                    turquoise sea.

Leeza Hodge (9)
Darite Primary School, Liskeard

My Magic Box
(Based on 'Magic Box' by Kit Wright)

I will put in my box . . .
The taste of sweet sugary strawberries at a tasty Sunday dinner,
A chunk of crunchy pineapple,
Chocolate melting in my mouth.

I will put in my box . . .
The oily smell of black petrol at the packed petrol station,
Freshly mown green grass,
Clothes fresh out of the washing machine.

I will put in my box . . .
The flash and crackle of white lightning streaming through the dark sky
                                              on a raging rainy day,
A firework going *bang* on Bonfire Night,
Ronaldinho showing off his cheeky tricks.

I will put in my box . . .
The feel of a firm football balancing on my small foot on a scorching
                                              summer day,
The hard, cool ground pressing against my back,
The cat's fluffy hair brushing against my hand.

My box is designed from ice, ogre bogies and silky rabbit hairs.
It is covered in bright blue splendid sapphires,
With a couple of glistening red rubies thrown in.
Its hinges are mighty God's huge toenail clippings.

I shall play football in my box
In Germany's biggest stadium.
I will score the winning goal
Lift the World Cup and every England fan will carry me away
Into the dead of night.

Ben Ackland (9)
Darite Primary School, Liskeard

My Magic Box
(Based on 'Magic Box' by Kit Wright)

I will put in my box . . .
The smooth, soft carpet on a cold winter night,
A brown, tubby bear on a wide, purple, pointy bed,
A soft, long, furry, purple piece of velvet creeping out of the basket.

I will put in my box . . .
The taste of long, black, thin, tasty piece of liquorice on a hot summer day.
A crumbly, crunchy and tasty chocolate biscuit fresh out of the tin,
Some chewy, soft and multicoloured marshmallows over a warm fire.

I will put in my box . . .
The fresh, clean clothes just coming out of the machine,
Fatty, salty, smelly bacon frying in a pan,
Long, tasty, saucy pasta being served slowly.

I will put in my box . . .
A clear, clean, blue, bright sky on a hot morning,
The squeaking of a rusty swing on a super summer's day,
A big blue rattle being shaken by a baby in a cot.

My box is designed from fairy's wings, silky cloth and multicoloured tissue.
There are pods of nectar from exotic, exquisite sunflowers on the lid.
It has giant's eyelashes for hinges.

I shall play basketball in my box
On the new London pitch then win the final game.
I will be on the news for everyone to see.
Then be carried off the pitch by all the team.

Gemma Wilkinson (8)
Darite Primary School, Liskeard

My Magic Box
(Based on 'Magic Box' by Kit Wright)

I will put in my box . . .
The smell of fragile flowers' nectar drunk by a beautiful butterfly,
In the grassy garden on a sunny day.

I will put in my box . . .
The taste of a sweet, sour pineapple,
Sitting in my lazy living room on the 5th of May.

I will put in my box . . .
Newborn baby calves just learning how to walk on a spring afternoon.

I will put in my box . . .
A soft, silky hamster scrambling along the rough carpet on a dark,
gloomy night.

My box is made of deer skin coloured dark brown with cream spots
On top of its back.
Its hinges are the finest red silk from the biggest country in the world,
Russia.

In my box
I will go to the beach on a nice hot day
And jump in my boat and sail away.
When I see a dolphin I will hop on its back,
Then swim away until the sky is black.

Beth Lewis (8)
Darite Primary School, Liskeard

My Magic Box
(Based on 'Magic Box' by Kit Wright)

I will put in my box . . .
A zoom of a zooming Ferrari,
A screech of a skidding Mercedes as it drives around the massive
                                                              echoing car park.

I will put in my box . . .
A bouncing squeak of a big Beetle's tyre as it falls off the
                                                              Liskeard road.

I will put in my box . . .
A sweet taste of a chocolate pudding sitting in a bowl ready to
                                                              be eaten.

I will put in my box . . .
A monkey swinging through the jungle on a summer morning.

I will put in my box
A broken engine from a motorbike rusting in my garage.

My box is made of a light jay bird's feather.
On the top sits a big, white, sparkly flower.

In my box
I would race in a Ferrari with the famous racers and win a huge
                                                              golden trophy.

Jacob Ferguson (8)
Darite Primary School, Liskeard

My Magic Box
(Based on 'Magic Box' by Kit Wright)

I will put in my box . . .
The smell of hot chocolate,
Cake sitting on a cooling tray,
The smell of carrot cake in the kitchen.

I will put in my box . . .
The soft fur of my rabbit,
The feel of my newly brushed hair after it has been washed.

I will put in my box . . .
A fat, black, calm, creeping cat from outside the dusty door.

My box is carved from wood of the tallest oak tree.

What I would do in my box is . . .
I would discover King Tut's jewels and I would play with my big sister
And I would watch Scooby-Doo on TV.

Sophie Tazzar (8)
Darite Primary School, Liskeard

The Black Widow

The black widow is . . .
Death.
It tiptoes silently and quickly,
A stealth specialist on a mission,
Sharp fangs . . .
Dripping with lethal venom.
Two teeth like syringes,
Injecting its helpless prey with death juice,
An evil, pocket-sized body,
An ability to kill instantly.
This makes it the black widow,
The most feared creature on the planet.

Dylan Peel (11)
Darite Primary School, Liskeard

The Magic Box
(Based on 'Magic Box' by Kit Wright)

I will put in my box . . .
A dog sitting by the fire keeping warm,
Until one of the sparks spits a flame and I hear my dog barking.

I will put in my box . . .
The hardest chocolate.
It tastes like sweet rock on a cold summer night.

I will put in my box . . .
Looking up to the sky and seeing two clouds crashing together.

I will put in my box . . .
The big, hot bonfire.
When you touch a spark it feels like hot, fast dust coming on you.

My box is made of stars and paint which is blue.
The hinges are like X-ray stars and inside it is rich red.

Sammy Vine (9)
Darite Primary School, Liskeard

Refugees

R unning away from their homes, they did not do it for fun
   they were forced to run away
E mpty stomachs rumbling away, there is not enough food to share
   between them all
F reedom does not exist in refugee camps, it takes so long
   to get wherever they need to go
U nderstanding what it is like to be a refugee, it is far too hard
                                 to imagine
G uns and bombs chased people away from their lovely, old homes
E veryone is walking with bare, dirty, cold feet, carrying bags of
   their belongings
E ating small amounts of food, trying to stay alive, but it is not easy
                                        at all
S melly, mouldy blankets are too rotten to sleep under,
   they need soft, cosy beds.

Ellie Doidge (10)
Denbury Primary School, Newton Abbot

Refugees

R agged, cut and patched-up clothes
E mpty lives and empty stomachs
F orced to leave their own homes
U nwanted lives and horrible homes
G uns flying up and bombs speeding down
E veryone running away to find a safer place
E ntering a world of fear, come refugees
S uffering adults and weeping children need our help!

Abby Foster-Turner (10)
Denbury Primary School, Newton Abbot

Refugee

R ugged rags draped around desperate bodies
E mpty houses left unwanted
F ar away from relatives and homes
U nder attack from bombing planes
G roups travel to find shelter
E veryone flees and nobody's left behind
E ating nothing for days on end.

Ed Roberts (11)
Denbury Primary School, Newton Abbot

Refugees

R efugees have wrecked houses to live in at the moment!
E mpty houses refugees live in, it's about to stop!
F reedom for refugees, they deserve it!
U nited, with destroyed homes unfortunately!
G uns are heard a lot by refugees!
E veryone gets home apart from refugees!
E nter nice house, we do but not refugees!

Guy Bennett (10)
Denbury Primary School, Newton Abbot

Refugee

R unning from the bombs, hiding round the corner
E ating from the rubbish cans, starving and hungry
F rightened and scared, hiding from everyone,
  Even the bombs, *Run! Run! Run!*
U nhappy child looking for his mum. *Frightened! Frightened! Frightened!*
G uns shooting at people, dying in front of you
E ating food with diseases in it
E veryone walking away from their homes.

Hayley Wakefield (10)
Denbury Primary School, Newton Abbot

Refugee

R ugged rags draped around desperate bodies
E ating and drinking is what refugees dream of
F riends and family is what refugees need
U nited as they trek hundreds of miles to safety
G roups travel wearily day and night
E veryone helps each other on the long, painful journey
E ntering a safe place at the end of their journey makes
                                            refugees happy.

Daniel Ponsford (10)
Denbury Primary School, Newton Abbot

Refugee

R efugees are forced to flee but that's where we come in
E mpty stomachs is all they feel
F reedom is all they dream of day and night
U nforgettable terrors they have to go through
G uns firing, bombs being dropped, means refugees having to flee
E gypt to Brazil is an example of how far they have to travel
E nergy is all they want to help them on their journey.

David Broughton (10)
Denbury Primary School, Newton Abbot

Help!

R ugged, wearing rags all day, no place to call home
E very refugee has to walk for weeks, maybe months barefoot
F orced to leave their homes
U niting with their family would be nice for them
G rabbing their most favourite things when forced to leave their homes
E mpty tummies waiting to be filled
E very day they think they are nearer to a new life.

Rebecca Kane (10)
Denbury Primary School, Newton Abbot

Refugees

R unning away, getting away from the war
E ating nothing for days on end
F eeling hungry, feeling sad
U nderage children running for help and freedom
G enerous people let refugees into their homes
E veryone suffering, waiting for some help
E ndless walking through deserts and sand
S earching for homes and people for friends.

Meah Howlett (10)
Denbury Primary School, Newton Abbot

Refugees

R ugged
E ver alone
F orever
U nder threat
G uns
E very day hungry
E ven
S tarving.

Timothy Mawson (10)
Denbury Primary School, Newton Abbot

Refugee

R unning away from death
E ating only leaves
F ighting for their lives
U nfortunate enough to have to give up their homes
G uns fire around the city
E veryone flees from the bombs
E ndless walking for days on end.

Tessa Burgin (10)
Denbury Primary School, Newton Abbot

Refugees

R ugged rags and no fresh air
E mpty houses and black ditches
F amilies dying and not much food
U nderground holes for homes
G uns going *bang! Bang!*
E verybody home but not the refugees
E nemy planes bombing the road.

Harvey Woodfield (10)
Denbury Primary School, Newton Abbot

Refugees

R agged
E mpty
F rightened
U nfortunate
G uns and bombs
E verybody starving
E verybody moving
S cared and abandoned.

Oliver Quant (10)
Denbury Primary School, Newton Abbot

Refugees

Running every day, in
    Rags, scared and afraid
Every day they are near to death, they need to
    Escape from pain, from running
Freedom is what they really want
    Fearing that they could be killed at any time
Under deep pressure they still fight
    Under all the rags there is a person
Grieving the dead, crying themselves to sleep
    Growing weaker every second
Eating lovely food and
    Everybody safe with no more worries
Shattered dreams, broken hearts, needing
    Schools, homes and love.

Jemima Richards (10)
Denbury Primary School, Newton Abbot

Refugee

R agged, struggling for a home,
    R   avenous for food
E mpty stomach with no food at all,
    E   mpty, begging all the way
F rightened of fierce, cruel animals,
    F   ighting for life
U nderstanding the hardness of life,
    U   nseen most of the time
G reedy families do not share,
    G   rabbing food everywhere
E ating small amounts
    E   very day, every night
E verywhere families struggle,
    E   veryone is sad.

Amy Pike & Paige Hammond (10)
Denbury Primary School, Newton Abbot

Refugees

R ugged rags wrapped all around people
   R ummaging in their rucksacks
E mpty, cold homes
   E veryone leaving barefoot
F ar, far away, freedom is waiting
   F ood is waiting too
U nderstanding what refugees are in the
   U nited Kingdom
G uns firing at hungry, poor people
   G oing home
E veryone eating happily, everybody
   E ating, nobody starving
E ntering the kingdom
   E verybody happy and pleased.

Eleanor Hughes (10)
Denbury Primary School, Newton Abbot

Refugees

R ags hang from the poor as they
   R un for their lives
E mpty inside, nowhere
   E lse to go
F ailing to get anywhere
   F ar, far away
U nder shelters to sleep and can't
   U nderstand why it's them
G uns, bombs going off
   G rown-ups and children dying
E verywhere, poor people
   E veryone should help
E ven when
   E veryone else is safe, they run
S urviving without water, they feed on
   S craps.

Lara Cosford (10)
Denbury Primary School, Newton Abbot

Refugees

R efugees do not have a happy life because they keep on moving
To refugee camps and walking miles
E ndless walking for refugees and endless moving barefoot over
Deserts and things
F un lives for refugees, not poverty for them
U n-dirty food would make them happy and no diseases
G etting toys not broken toys for them
E ndless comfort for them
E ating clean and nice food for them.

Michael Bennett (10)
Denbury Primary School, Newton Abbot

Refugees

R efugees hoping for a good life, not one with poverty
E asier lives are all they want just like us!
F un lives, not boring lives
This is their dream
U nited with family who are at war, seeing them at last
G etting nice toys to play with, not broken ones
E ating food which isn't just scraps.
E ating food which is good for them, at least to let them live.
S leeping at night with no guns going off.

Michael Langler (11)
Denbury Primary School, Newton Abbot

My Cat

Once I had a cat called Glossy
When I got home she was very bossy
She played in the pool
And was always a fool
But I loved her
Lots and lots!

Lauren Goldsmith (10)
Ernesettle Community School, Plymouth

My Teddies

Once I had a teddy called Flossy
When she came alive, she was a bit bossy
All my teddies upon my bed
Sometimes jumped upon my head
One day Flossy said
To stop jumping upon her head.

I woke up one day
All my teddies were up and away
Flossy said to me
'I didn't think you were going to wake up today.'

Zoe Clark (10)
Ernesettle Community School, Plymouth

The Headless Teddy

My mate Fred,
Has got a ted,
On his bed,
He's got no head,
Because it was my friend Ned,
That chopped it off,
Now it's in the shed,
Ted is dead.

Ben Ellis (10)
Ernesettle Community School, Plymouth

My Teddy Bear, Clair

Once I had
A teddy bear
Called Clair
Who had a lot
Of fluffy hair
Whose head looked
Like a pear!

Mollie Neale (10)
Ernesettle Community School, Plymouth

Butterflies Flying Everywhere

Butterflies flying everywhere
Does anyone care?
Beautiful wings, how many eyes?
Two on the back to scare other animals in disguise
Butterflies flying everywhere
Does anyone care?

Then one day someone said
'Look at the butterfly
With multicoloured wings
It flew away, someone said
There are plenty more beautiful butterflies alive.

Does anyone care?
Some people care
Then one day, beautiful butterflies flew down
Everyone said, 'Butterflies are beautiful'
Does anyone care?
Everyone cares!

Kieran Cadman (10)
Ernesettle Community School, Plymouth

My Best Friend

My best friend is Connor Menhenick
He is a really good friend
He has a lot of fun
He has a bun
And likes sports
And has never seen dwarfs
When he is mad
He shouts at his dad!

Daniel May (10)
Ernesettle Community School, Plymouth

The Safari

In the wild
The heat is mild
Animals are hiding
People are riding
Safari vans
Drinking from Coca-Cola cans

Cheetahs are running
The view is stunning
Safari is fun
Under the shining sun
The tigers are hard to see
For both you and me

The cheetahs are running fast
And the time is going past
The sun is going down
And everyone's starting to frown
The safari was fun.

Kimberly Nathan (10)
Ernesettle Community School, Plymouth

Firefly

I open my jar
And then,
I catch a firefly,
It's trying to escape!

All of a sudden,
The light goes out
And I realise, I've killed it!
I hate this moment!
I only watch the firefly,
From now on,
Flying in the air, *free!*

Natalie Bone (10)
Ernesettle Community School, Plymouth

Flower Seeds, Growing Bees

Flower seeds, growing bees
Lighting up the sky
Mother Nature begins to cry
Then she starts to fly

Insects grow, water flows
Sun shines from up high
What a beautiful day
To be alive

Beehives anywhere
Any tree, everywhere
All you can see is honey and bees
When the light shines down on me.

Shawnee Redding (10)
Ernesettle Community School, Plymouth

Summertime

S ummer is bright
U nlike winter, when you have to wrap up tight
M ilk, strawberry and mint ice cream
M akes you feel like you're in a dream
E veryone's on the beach
R unning and eating a great big peach
T ime to plant some seeds
I t's time to dig out the weeds
M y garden's clean now
E ven when the sun goes down.

Harlie Uren (10)
Ernesettle Community School, Plymouth

Animals In The Summer

Stormy seas, buzzing bees
Brightening up the sky
They speed their way
Along the day
And don't take any notice
What is coming their way

Swimming dolphins
Hammerhead sharks
Dolphins are nice
Unlike sharks
Dolphins are very smart
Unlike the swimming shark.

Daniel Davies (10)
Ernesettle Community School, Plymouth

My Three Best Friends

My three best friends
Are Meghan, Kimberly and Gemma
We are really clever
And always hang together
We're always on the move
We like to party and groove.

My three best friends
Are Meghan, Kimberly and Gemma
We are the best friends forever
We're always in the sunny weather
My three best friends
Are Meghan, Kimberly and Gemma!

Kathryn Hammond (10)
Ernesettle Community School, Plymouth

Like A Fairy Tale

You could try and make me sob and cry
I'd like to see you try and try
Because just like in a fairy tale
I'm the dragon, flying high.

Do my gentle ways hurt you bad?
Do you want to have detention?
'Cause just like a pretty princess
I'm the centre of attention.

You can burn me with your curries
Or just tell me all your worries
Don't worry, I am kind
You'll never get left behind.

You could tangle my hair up
And make me cry about it
But just like in a fairy tale
I'm the pink, cuddly rabbit.

Just like in a fairy tale
Yes, just like in a fairy tale
Just like in a fairy tale
I'm the dragon, flying high.

Flying high, flying high, flying high!

Lauren Jenkins (10)
Hannah More Primary School, Bristol

Still I Shine

You may diss me with your horrid words
Hurt me with your looks
You may beat me with your gang so fine
But still, like an angel, I will shine

Does my intelligence upset you?
Why are you looking so ashamed?
'Cause I know how to use my smartness
At any time of day

Just like stars, just like the sun
Light burning hot like fire
Just like the brightness beating down on me
I will shine

You may tell me about my looks
Compare me to you crooks
You may shout and scream all you like
You may even ride my bike
You may exclude me from your games
And I won't even hope it rains.

I will shine, I will shine, I will shine!

Wadzani Mukambirwa (10)
Hannah More Primary School, Bristol

I Care

You may push me into doing things
That I really hate, not like
You may make me sell all my toys
But not my favourite bike

Does my lack of jealousy upset you?
Just 'cause I'm not like you
I don't have to obey your every rule
And do what you tell me to do

Just like you and like me
We are all human beings
But you're the one acting crazy
I don't know what you are seeing

You may drive me down to Blackmail Street
Make me feel so trapped and scared
You may beat me, kick me, neck-back me
But my friends will come, they care.

I care, they care, I care!

Seanique Reuben (9)
Hannah More Primary School, Bristol

I'll Come Like Night

You may trick me with your dirty words
With all your might and fright
You may beat me up with all your gang
But still I'll come, like the night.

Does my loveliness make you jealous?
Why do you look like you're in pain?
I am everyone's dreams and hopes
I will come, like the night, again and again.

Excuse me, Mr Bully Boy,
What have you been saying?
You haven't seen what I have seen
Even though we're both human beings.

You may scratch me for the rest of my life,
With your words like a knife you will cause me strife,
You may cut me with a razor knife,

I'll come like the night, I'll come like the night, I'll come like the night!

Layla Henry Smith (10)
Hannah More Primary School, Bristol

Still, Like A Warrior, I Will Fight

You may batter me into the earth
With your words and daggers of the night
You may stab me in my very heart
But still, like a warrior, I will fight.

Does my powerfulness make you jealous?
Why do you always try?
No matter, no matter just how much
You'll never make me cry.

Just like cats and like dogs
Fighting with all their might
Just like cats chasing mice
Like a warrior, I will fight.

You may cheat me from now until I die
You may not let me out of your sight
Trample me with hate and hope I surrender
But still, like a warrior, I'll fight.

I'll fight, I'll fight, I'll fight!

Emily Richer (10)
Hannah More Primary School, Bristol

Still I Shine

You may tell your lies about me
Because you're filled with jealousy
Still, like the sun, I shine.

Does my happiness upset you?
Why are you so angry?
'Cause I'm happy with me
Not sad like you are with you?

Just like tide and like clouds
And the sun that's shining high
I will shine.

You may cut me with your temper
You may kill me with your words
You may hurt me with your bitter ways
But still, I will shine.

Still I shine, still I shine, still I shine!

Declan Batt (10)
Hannah More Primary School, Bristol

Still, Like Cats, I Land On My Feet

You may chew me like a piece of meat
You may pop me like a balloon
But still, like cats, I land on my feet

Does my beauty make you jealous?
Why are you so glum?
'Cause I ate the last fish and your exquisite bun?

Just like cats, just like dogs
Going round and round in circles
Still, like cats, I land on my feet

You may hang me by my skinny neck
Or put me on a royal throne
You may call me a dreaded freak
But still, like cats, I land on my feet

I land on my feet, I land on my feet, I land on my feet!

Alyssa Small (9)
Hannah More Primary School, Bristol

Still Like Stars, I Glow

You may exclude me from your games
And use abusive words to my face
Like broken glass bottles
But still, like stars, I glow

Does my happiness offend you?
Why are you so sad and lonely?
'Cause I smile like I'm the happiest person
On this Earth?

Just like butterflies fly high
Still, like stars, I glow

You may punch me with your words
You may blackmail me, you know
But still, like stars, I glow.

I glow, I glow, I glow!

Dean Eatwell (10)
Hannah More Primary School, Bristol

Still I'll Flow

You may strangle me with your awful words
Blackmail me with your hate
You may mark me down from ten to one
But still, like water, I will flow.

Does my beautiful face upset you?
Why are you crying like a baby?
'Cause I eat like I'm excited
And as happy as can be?

Just like food and drink
Just like winds blowing by
Still, I'll flow.

You may pull my hair with your big stick
You may bruise me with stones
You may hurt me with stinging nettles
But still, like clouds, I'll flow.

I'll flow, I'll flow, I'll flow!

Daniel Millin (10)
Hannah More Primary School, Bristol

Trees

Trees swift in the air like birds gliding
They turn a light brown in the autumn
Trees turn green in the sun
Children play and climb the trees
While the bark comes off slowly

Winter comes, trees turn white
People play in the snow
The trees return to normal
Trees turn green and children play as normal
Leaves turn brown, fall down
And they come out as empty trees.

George Mole (10)
Nailsworth CE Primary School, Nailsworth

The Moon

The moon twinkled as I looked through my telescope
Something struck me as I looked
There were illuminations reflecting
On the moon.

There were people moving, bouncing on the moon
I sat and watched the little people
Sprawling around on the moon
Going in different directions.

I saw a rocket, people started to load into it
I watched it start its engine
The rocket took off, illuminating the moon
With the flames of the engine.

It flew past the stars and past Mercury
And all of the other eight planets
To my surprise, the rocket disappeared
Beyond the twinkling stars.

Jade Lefeuvre (10)
Nailsworth CE Primary School, Nailsworth

Dennis The Dog

Dennis gets up
Goes in the garden
Has a fight with Molly
Goes in Katy's room
Gets on the bed
And sleeps.

Dennis gets up
He meets Billy the rabbit
Runs away
Gets on the trampoline
Dennis' belly rumbles
Dennis eats
And sleeps.

Jack Newman (9)
Nailsworth CE Primary School, Nailsworth

Buddy The Budgie

Buddy wakes up,
Tweets for food,
Tweets for water,
Annoys everybody just for fun
Watches the news,
Plucks his feathers and sleeps.

Buddy wakes up,
Cuts through his cage,
Climbs on a toy car,
Plays and carries on.

Buddy scares himself
In the bathroom mirror,
Plays on a toy ladder,
Eats and sleeps.

Buddy wakes up,
Eats, drinks a lot of water,
Climbs on the dog's bed
And sleeps for the whole night . . .
Almost!

Sara Tasnim (10)
Nailsworth CE Primary School, Nailsworth

Rose The Horse

Rose gallops around in the field,
Eats some grass,
Has a fight with Harvey,
Makes friends with others,
Has a race against another,
Does her business and sleeps,
Next day she makes a date with Ginger,
Chases her tail,
Jumps on her back legs
And makes a really loud noise.

Jasmine Rosser (10)
Nailsworth CE Primary School, Nailsworth

Coco, The Guinea Pig

Coco wakes up, eats,
Jumps maniac-like
And then sleeps.
Coco wakes up,
Eats dandelion leaves,
Jumps through his tube
And sleeps.
Coco wakes up,
Eats,
Jumps in his house,
Comes back out,
Goes to the toilet,
Jumps on his house
And sleeps.
Coco wakes up,
Eats his food,
Squeaks in his cage,
Year 5 hear him
And he sleeps.
Coco wakes up,
Has a drink,
Eats some food
And sleeps.
Coco wakes up,
Has cuddles with Year 5
And sleeps.
Coco wakes up,
Scratches himself,
Runs around his cage,
Dives through his tube.
And sleeps.

Luke Daniels (10)
Nailsworth CE Primary School, Nailsworth

Alfie The Dog

Alfie wakes up
Mum takes him out
Comes back
Drinks
Jumps around in the garden
Comes in
Cleans himself
Sleeps.

Alfie wakes up
Gets his toy
Plays with it
Goes in the garden
Does his business
Eats and sleeps.

Mum comes in from work
Takes Alfie out
Mum brings him back
Alfie chases next-door's cat
Goes and plays with next-door's dog
Comes home
And sleeps.

Alfie wakes up
Has a drink
Chases his tail
Goes out into the garden
Licks a dead mouse
Comes in
Has a drink
Eats a treat
And sleeps.

Megan Farrer (10)
Nailsworth CE Primary School, Nailsworth

What Coco Does

Coco wakes up,
Runs around a lot,
Eats and sleeps.

Coco wakes up,
Watches children working,
Eats and sleeps.

Coco wakes up,
Escapes out of the cage,
Steals the teacher's cuppa,
Goes back into the cage,
Eats and sleeps.

Coco wakes up,
Watches the OHP,
Finds a private place,
In the cage,
Eats and sleeps.

Coco has hobbies,
Watching children working,
Eating the display
And squeaking at the teacher.

Coco wakes up
Bites the chubby fingers,
Eats and sleeps.

Jacob Elliot Harris (10)
Nailsworth CE Primary School, Nailsworth

Bubbles

Bubbles wakes up
Swims around,
Plays with whatever,
Flaps his fin at Spike
And sleeps.

Bubbles wakes up,
Does a backflip,
Eats some food
And sleeps.

Bubbles wakes up,
Plays with Spike and Peter,
Blows bubbles at whatever
And sleeps.

Bubbles wakes up,
Hides in the plants
And sleeps.

Bubbles wakes up,
Swims around the pond
And sleeps.

Bubbles is my goldfish,
And he normally sleeps.

Henrietta Ruby Davis (10)
Nailsworth CE Primary School, Nailsworth

Eddy The Dog

Monday
Eddy wakes up,
Chases the horses in the field,
Comes indoors,
Eats,
Finds a private place in the garden
And sleeps.

Tuesday
Eddy wakes up,
Comes upstairs,
Licks my feet,
Goes downstairs,
Does his business in the hedges,
Comes indoors,
Has a drink
And sleeps.

Wednesday
Eddy wakes up,
Has some chocolate (uh-oh),
Goes to sleep,
Wakes up,
Vomits on the carpet
And sleeps.

Thursday
Eddy wakes up,
Eats and sleeps.

Friday
Eddy wakes up,
Plays tug of war with me,
Eats and sleeps.

Jack Sessions (10)
Nailsworth CE Primary School, Nailsworth

Abby The Cat

Abby wakes up,
Goes outside,
Stalks a mouse,
Eats,
Does her business
And sleeps.

Abby wakes up,
Comes indoors,
Covers herself in spit,
Eats
And sleeps.

Abby wakes up,
Rolls on the floor,
Has a catnap,
Wakes up,
Eats
And sleeps.

Abby wakes up,
Eats
And sleeps.

Abby wakes up,
Does her business,
Sits on the doormat,
Eats
And sleeps.

Declan Scott (10)
Nailsworth CE Primary School, Nailsworth

Five Days In The Life Of A Hamster

Tangle wakes up,
Inflates her pouches,
Stinks out the corner,
Deflates her pouches
And sleeps.

Tangle wakes up,
Has a fight with her bedding,
Stinks out her corner,
Spins in her wheel
And sleeps.

Tangle wakes up,
Crashes into the wall in her ball,
Makes a date with Fudge,
Stinks out the corner
And sleeps.

Tangle wakes up,
Stinks out the corner,
Tastes a human sausage,
Eats
And sleeps.

Tangle wakes up,
Stinks out the corner,
Daydreams about Fudge,
Shares a Malteser with Fudge
And sleeps.

Milly Griffin (10)
Nailsworth CE Primary School, Nailsworth

What Tabby Does

Tabby wakes up
Runs around the house
Licks my mum's face
I feed him
He goes outside
Runs around the garden
And sleeps.

Tabby wakes up
Goes outside
Catches mice
And sleeps.

Tabby wakes up
Jumps in the toilet
Eats
And sleeps.

Tabby wakes up
Fights with me
And sleeps.

Tabby wakes up
Plays with Charlie
Eats
And sleeps.

Marcus Shortland (10)
Nailsworth CE Primary School, Nailsworth

What Tangle Does

Tangle wakes up
Eats her broccoli
Runs around the cage
And sleeps.

Tangle wakes up
Goes to the toilet
And sleeps.

Tangle wakes up
Runs around
And sleeps.

Tangle wakes up
Plays in her wheel
Eats some more
And sleeps.

Tangle wakes up
Stinks out the corner
Bites my finger
Begs for more food
And sleeps.

Tangle wakes up
Gets scared by Tatti
And sleeps.

Ben Wear (10)
Nailsworth CE Primary School, Nailsworth

Tea

Tea,
Tea,
Tea,
Mrs Dougill loves tea,
Strawberry tea,
Blackberry tea,
Mint tea,
Blueberry tea,
Book tea,
Dip-your-biscuit-in tea,
Mrs Dougill's tea.

Tea,
Tea,
Tea,
There are many types of tea,
Plum tea,
Apple tea,
Mango tea,
Lemon tea,
Coffee tea,
Home-made tea,
Bought-from-the-shop tea,
And the last one
The tea that isn't even tea!

Eleanor Kate Milner (10)
Nailsworth CE Primary School, Nailsworth

Freddy The Frog

Freddy the frog eats
Asks Danny the dog out
Has a fight with Flanders
Eats and sleeps.

Freddy wakes up
Eats flies
Finds a place on a lilypad
Eats and sleeps.

Freddy wakes up
Eats
Has a fight with Ginger
Eats and sleeps.

Freddy wakes up
Eats, plays with his toys
Eats and sleeps.

Harry Dowdeswell (9)
Nailsworth CE Primary School, Nailsworth

A Day Out

One sunny morning down in the park
Glen goes for a run around the track
He sees his friend sitting quietly on the bench.

One sunny morning down in the park
Glen saw a swan gliding in the air
Reaching into his pocket
He pulled out a loaf of bread
Suddenly, the ducks quacked all around him.

Callum Gainey (10)
Nailsworth CE Primary School, Nailsworth

Fred The Deinychus

Fred eats
Hangs out with his pack
Wanders around
Has a fight with Al the Allosaurus
And sleeps.

Fred wakes up
Kills an Iguanodon
Eats
Finds a private place
Sharpens his claws
And sleeps.

Fred wakes up
Checks for dinosaurs
Checks for lizards
Checks for birds
Kills an Edmontosaurus
Eats and sleeps.

Jason Jones (10)
Nailsworth CE Primary School, Nailsworth

Steven's Magic

Steven opened the creaky wooden door
And a shocking light shone
It went pitch-black and Steven walked forward
He fell down a dark hole
And it was blue and gold shiny stuff
And he landed on a heap of jewels
He was in the land of the rainbow forest.

Terri Ann Smith-Gardiner (9)
Nailsworth CE Primary School, Nailsworth

Summer!

Summer is fun!
You have a barbeque -
Enjoy the burger buns,
Then go in the pool.
In the nearby field,
The cows are going *moo,*
In the pool, Natalie keeps cool.

Mum shouts, 'Barbeque's ready!'
William thinks the chicken's tasty,
Laura thinks the sausages are yummy!
My dad is swimming,
My mum is cutting lemons.

Emma and Jade turn up in their bikinis -
Jacob turns up in his trunks.
Summer is really fun!
Messing around in the sun!
Summer is the best season ever!

Gemma Mansell (9)
Rushall CE Primary School, Pewsey

My Dream Horse

My dream horse would be Millie,
She's a big and gentle Shire,
So calm and good,
Just like she should.
She's a pretty piebald -
All black and white at 14.2hh,
She's only two,
But acts like she's ten.
She loves to jump,
Hacking as well,
She's as soft as anything.
So now you can plainly see -
This is why I love Millie!

Bethany Smith (10)
Rushall CE Primary School, Pewsey

Teachers

'Get on with your work!'
Shouted the green toad in the corner,
While she went into the cupboard
And then a *ginormous green monster* . . . came out,
With a red, hairy back,
'Argh . . . !' screamed the children
And they ran to the headmaster's office,
But little did they know that he was in a dress!

The next day the children went back to school,
They were very scared, but they braved it,
She was sat in the corner, just waiting till they came in,
But she had destroyed the room . . .
What had happened?
You're not going to know . . . !

Alice Spanswick (10)
Rushall CE Primary School, Pewsey

My Sister From Mars

Brothers and sister don't get on,
Especially me and my sister.
At 11.30 she changes into a Martian,
I'm actually quite scared, she's nasty!

I can't wait until 1.30,
I'm finishing my bacon.
I hear a loud *boom!*
And she goes walking into my room.

It's her! She always looks the same,
Tall, ugly and slimy green,
A storm is brewing, I'm scared!

Don't worry, this poem is only a joke!

Dominic Tandy (10)
Rushall CE Primary School, Pewsey

Camping Out

At the moment it's wind and rain,
We're waiting for a break,
So we can make plans to go camping,
I can't wait!

When the weather is warmer
And we don't get too wet,
We will put on our rucksacks
And pack our camouflage nets.
It's the woods on the plains,
Where we'll be sneaking about,
And eating outside - camping's such fun,
I can't wait!

We'll be camping outside,
Living like soldiers, testing ourselves,
Out world on our shoulders,
Our pots, our pans, our tent.
We've got all we need to keep us going,
But we will visit the villages,
For our fresh food and water -
It's a challenge I'll love,
I can't wait!

Sam Flippance (8)
Rushall CE Primary School, Pewsey

Homework

Homework is good,
Homework is bad.
When I am finished,
I am so glad.

Literacy, numeracy,
Science and art.
I'd rather be eating,
A sticky jam tart!

I can't afford,
A private tutor.
I'm trying to save up,
For a great big computer!

I begin with my pencil,
My rubber and my pad
And jot down the answers
To make teacher glad.

She sighs with relief,
When I hand it in -
And looks at my answers
With a big, smiley grin.

Jamie Russell (10)
Rushall CE Primary School, Pewsey

Cats

Cats find somewhere warm
Cats are lazy on the bed
Cats are very cosy
Cats are soft
Cats are hunters and killers
Cats kill birds, rabbits and mice
Cats go off to the woods
To hunt the animals
Cats are playful and play with their toys
And play around with me
Cats play with the dog and miaow too
Cats are crazy when they are ginger
Cats have feelings
When they are upset or hungry
And scratch at the door
When they want to go out
All cats are *purrrrrrrfect!*

Chloe Beaven (10)
Rushall CE Primary School, Pewsey

Teachers

Teachers, teachers, creepy creatures,
They have very ugly features.
They send shivers down your spine,
When they walk into the room,
They make the classroom look like a dungeon of doom.
There's sickly science teacher who smells of smelly socks,
There's the angry English teacher who wears frilly frocks,
There's the mad maths teacher who moans about me,
There's the horrid history teacher who has a pet flea,
They all sit in the staffroom drinking large cups of tea
And those are the teachers that really scare me!

Laura Tyley (11)
Rushall CE Primary School, Pewsey

My Cat

My cat is very furry
And very, very soft.
She is always very fluffy
And she sleeps up in my loft.

She's a big, beautiful tabby cat,
She's white, black and grey.
She attacks my furry mat,
As she plays with her stuffed rat.

She's very cute and sleepy,
She mopes about the house.
But when she is not doing this,
She tries to catch a mouse.

She is very slick and sly
And she runs very fast.
She is also very scatty,
As she comes whizzing past.

Zoe Spanswick (11)
Rushall CE Primary School, Pewsey

A Year Of Brothers

January's brother is a nightmare
February's brother is just as bad
March's brother is such a mess
April's brother has got a dress
May's brother is such a brat
June's brother smells like a rat
July's brother is such an animal
August's brother is a cheeky monkey
September's brother is number one minger
October's brother is from outer space
November's brother is such a big bully
December's brother is really a wally.

Jacob Garrett (9)
Rushall CE Primary School, Pewsey

Friends

Friends are always there for me,
Not matter what I say or do.
They like me for the way I am
And not because I'm someone I'm not.

With my friends I have laughs,
Go shopping for clothes
And see cinema shows,
Not to mention the odd rows.

The sleepovers I have are always great,
They are always with all my mates.
We play all games and what's the name
And then pretend that we have fame.

Kristan Menard (11)
Rushall CE Primary School, Pewsey

St Lucia The Great

S parkling clear ocean
T ropical rainforest and wildlife

L ovely vegetation
U nless in the city
C elebrate occasions
I mportant to the world
A big tourist attraction

S peaking people in the
T own, busy buzzing everywhere

L ike a blizzard through a bridge
U nderneath an evening sea
C hristians go to church
I ncredible beaches dotted around
A mazing landscapes can be found.

Gemma Ogden (9)
St Mary's CE (VA) Primary School, Portbury

Jamaica

J amaican people play steel drums
A nd it has great lakes to canoe on
M ango Bay happens
A loud drum gets hit there
I n the afternoon the sun sets high then low
C aribbean Sea, is where it lies
A t Jamaica this happens

J amaica, Jamaica
A n amazing sight every night, of a sunset
M arvellous food smells fill the air
A nd amazing things go on there
I n the forest, the Ocho Rios lake flows through
C entral City is really busy
A nd it's a beautiful place to be.

Peter Kearsley (8)
St Mary's CE (VA) Primary School, Portbury

Ecuador, Ecuador

E njoyable Ecuador
C apital city is Quito
U nbelievable mountains
A nd amazing animals
D rums make beautiful music
O r the bow played violin
R ed-breasted birds sing the best songs

E njoyable queen of Ecuador
C limate grows hot from her breath
U nbelievable jagged mountains poke the sky
A nd amazing pets of the queen
D rum makes the sun peep out
O r no music, she gets furious
R ed-breasted bird makes the queen dance away.

Thomas Scanlan (9)
St Mary's CE (VA) Primary School, Portbury

Mexico

M oon shining brightly
E specially at glowing night
eX tremely well made crafts that everyone buys
I ncredibly packed with people and soon they will meet
C limate cautiously blows like a whistle being played
O cean high, amazingly swift

M isty clouds float in the sky
E nthusiastic people chat quietly
eX tremely blinding sun
I ndigo seas clear the shore
C heerful people shake hands
O ther people buzz about to try to get to work

M ild wind blows in your face, how soft does it feel
E xcited people hop around
eX tremely good homes for everyone to stay
I n the night, wild animals are stalking their land
C ountry of Mexico is peeping round the world
O ther animals prance around flying

M ade crafts for everyone as they peep right around the corner
E xcitedly the countries meet and all the people jump
eX tremely friendly people
I n the day it's baking, as if you're in an oven
C an you see how hot it is in Mexico?
O f course, the weather changes every now and again!

Eleanor Grey (9)
St Mary's CE (VA) Primary School, Portbury

Latin America - Panama

P eople on the beach enjoying themselves all day long
A nd the birds singing nicely all the time
N o people not enjoying themselves
A nd lots of people seeing lovely animals there
M aybe it will be quiet soon
A nd it won't be long till it's quiet, people will be gone soon.

Kira Phillipou (7)
St Mary's CE (VA) Primary School, Portbury

Costa Rica, Costa Rica

C entral San José City, kind and peaceful
O ften some people go to the beach and
S ome people go on holiday to beautiful places
T alented people play music for money
A nd some people do it because they're poor

R are sights are very common as it comes to sunset
I t will come in ten more minutes
C alm seas brushing against the shore showing off their colours
A nd now it comes, the sunset falls and the dark blue sky appears

C alm Costa Rica, everyone having a great time
O ceans twist and crash on the shore
S eas yell and destroy the beach
T he wind spins and turns
A s the people just watch it

R ampaging twister flings itself on the beach
I t washes everything out of the way
C hairs fly and float in the air
A s the people open their eyes and realise it was just a dream.

Dan Steven (9)
St Mary's CE (VA) Primary School, Portbury

Venezuela

V ery pretty countryside Venezuela has
E xcellent tropical rainforests trickle through water paths
N aughty long-tailed monkeys swing from vine to vine
E verlasting trees are home to rare animals
Z igzag paths run through the mountains
U nder every leaf, a different coloured frog
E ach waterfall twinkles in the sunlight
L akes swarm with hungry crocodiles
A ll the streets of wonderful Venezuela have happy, smiling people.

Alice Robinson (9)
St Mary's CE (VA) Primary School, Portbury

Brasil

B eaming sun beats again
R ampaging through the city, the sun stays
A mazingly people beg
S un suddenly runs to you
I mmediately sun sets and starts to go down
L impingly, I run like a jaguar through the grass

B rasil is a wealthy place
R ich people don't mix with poor people
A sun peeps out
S un stays, it never goes down
I n the day people beg and wander
L ight is fading

B eaches hit the waves as they rest
R ampaging children play on the beaches all day
A mazingly they build sandcastles happily
S un hits the sand and makes it hot
I t has come to the end where the children go
L ight hits you.

Abbie Cooper (9)
St Mary's CE (VA) Primary School, Portbury

Chile

C reeping caterpillars crawl about
H igh Andes mountains stretch for the clouds
I ndustrious men dig for copper
L ittle llamas plod fields
E choes shout about the place

C hildren poor and children rich never meet on the streets in the
H ot weather
I cy icebergs freeze the sky
L ight snowflakes float to the ground
E legant sun rises at dawn.

Molly Cheek (7)
St Mary's CE (VA) Primary School, Portbury

Peru

P erfect sunset
E very time I see it I see
R ainbow-coloured smears
U nder the beautiful Peruvian sky

P eople strolling through Peru
E very city busy
R ound the corner comes a horse
U nder a heavy burden

P eople peep around as the sun comes out
E very face starts to smile
R ain has gone, the sun is out
U mbrellas are no longer seen or needed

P acific Ocean laps the white, sparkling sand
E l Niño
R uins the ocean and makes it rough. It
U psets the ocean and causes a drought.

Georgia Weekes (9)
St Mary's CE (VA) Primary School, Portbury

Costa Rica

C urious animals running out
O f breath and the beautiful trees
S wishing in the blowing wind
T hick grass glowing in the sun
A nd tiny little birds singing in the background

R ainforests camouflaged with the trees
I n the middle there is an amazing waterfall
C old and clean, smells like cold, fresh ice
A nd it just brightens up my life.

Ben Collins (9)
St Mary's CE (VA) Primary School, Portbury

Argentina

A mazing sunset at evening
R ivers flow gently through Argentina
G o to the wonderful waterfalls
E nter the incredible scenery
N ow enjoy the sun
T he tempest enfolds the day
I nfernos rage from Tierra del Fuego
N ever ever go to this wet and windy place
A s you leave Argentina, you look behind as flowers appear.

Rob Lange (9)
St Mary's CE (VA) Primary School, Portbury

St Lucia

S ome people try and rest when they are here
T o have tea and a break

L ooking at the gorgeous sky
U p amazingly high
C lear and shiny, lovely and warm
I t's lush and nice like sugar and spice
A nd don't forget, I will be there!

Georgia Ross (9)
St Mary's CE (VA) Primary School, Portbury

Ecuador

E cuador, Ecuador
C limate is boiling hot
U nbelievable jagged mountains
A nd scary animals
D readful houses
O r unbelievable shelters
R ainforests are amazing places to go.

Jack Edwards (9)
St Mary's CE (VA) Primary School, Portbury

Venezuela

V ery beautiful waterfalls they have
E veryone loves the waterfalls there
N otes of music are heard from the town
E very factory sells lots of oil
Z eus the god would have loved it here
U nder rocks there are creepy-crawlies
E nter each rainforest with fascination
L ots of bushes rolling against each other
A t the beach, you can see the slowing sunset sinking into the sea.

Emma Adamson (9)
St Mary's CE (VA) Primary School, Portbury

Peru

P retty sparkling yellow sun in the sky
E arly sunset at night, sinking down behind the cliffs
R ainforest-coloured sea
U nder the light blue sky

P eru, Peru, I love you
E very city packed
R ound the corner comes a running horse
U nder a crooked bridge.

Esme Pain (7)
St Mary's CE (VA) Primary School, Portbury

Bolivia

B olivia, Bolivia
O range sun sets in the evening
L ake Titicaca is the highest lake
I t is steaming hot and it can be very cold
V ery big llamas stroll across the road
I n Bolivia they grow fruit
A nd they grow coffee.

Megan Stephens (8)
St Mary's CE (VA) Primary School, Portbury

Carnival

C arnival is all around
A nd everyone is involved
R io de Janeiro is a-buzz with life
N ever could you see such a sight
I ndividuals wait for it all year round
V arious people spend more than a pound
A mazing sights to see everywhere
L ent is very near, so let's dance the night away!

Adam Grey (10)
St Mary's CE (VA) Primary School, Portbury

Mexico, Mexico

M ild wind blows in Mexico like a hot, drifting breath
E xcellent sweetcorn, some people are begging for it
eX tremely hot sun like a beaming torch
I n school is better than out on the street for Mexican children
C oncentrating when they finally get an education
O ther animals are dangerous, ours too,
    But I think they're mainly after you!

Georgia Oliver (7)
St Mary's CE (VA) Primary School, Portbury

A Carnival Poem!

C arnival people wandering the streets
A mazing costumes, great hats
R oaring music with steady beats
N ot any animals, but costumes of cats
I nside the markets, children laughing
V aluable jewels
A nd the fun is cracking
L oving, everyone is a laugh!

Emily Cosway (10)
St Mary's CE (VA) Primary School, Portbury

Waiting

C ounting the seconds before the moment
A mazing amounts of people just waiting
R unning along, pushing to get in
N ever letting yourself fall to the back
I ncredible noise comes from the crowd
V arious murmurs can be heard in the distance
A mazingly, the people become quiet
L aughter fills the air, then
S uddenly, you hear the music, it begins!

Paige Robinson (11)
St Mary's CE (VA) Primary School, Portbury

Carnival

C arnival has arrived
A wonderful atmosphere to be in
R io is full of colour
N obody is miserable
I love the sensational masks
V ibrant colours passing by
A lovely time of year
L eaving time, I am sad.

Alex Smith (10)
St Mary's CE (VA) Primary School, Portbury

Guyana

G uyana - echoing forests, crying leaves
U p in the trees, swinging parrots screeching like children
Y oung snakes hissing
A nd the busy towns house poor and rich
N ot a sound in the city
A ll the animals rustling in the forest.

Jake Wherlock (8)
St Mary's CE (VA) Primary School, Portbury

A Carnival Acrostic!

C arnivals are fabulous, carnivals are fun
A special time of year, has only just begun
R hino costumes, great celebrations
N ot to mention, the music's vibrations
I nvitation - you don't need one
V ibrating music, just have some fun
A nimal costumes, cheering and laughing
L ots of special carnival dancing!

Emily O'Hara (10)
St Mary's CE (VA) Primary School, Portbury

Carnival

C arnivals happen all over the world
A ll great headwear on parade
R ainbow colours on the costumes
N ew designs every year
I t looks fantastic
V ery loud samba music goes on and on
A nd lots of dancing
L ots of happy memories made.

Thomas Ryan (11)
St Mary's CE (VA) Primary School, Portbury

Carnival

C arnivals are for people to wonder
A mazing costumes for all to see
R azzamatazz and, lots of fun
N othing you couldn't miss
I nside the darkness brightened by costumes
V aluable headdresses, funny and amazing
A nd all so colourful, filled with excitement
L aughter and cheering all day long.

Leah Collins (10)
St Mary's CE (VA) Primary School, Portbury

Carnivals

Deep in Rio, carnivals go on
And lots of people celebrate and sing songs,
The headdresses are colourful and bright,
You just want to dance all night!
People make their own headdresses
To dance and impress,
Looking at the headdresses make people's eyes go blind!
And all the people are funny and all so kind!
Some headdresses are feathery and whacky
And they make lots of people feel happy!
Hear the music playing
And dance to the beat!
The music is loud and you can hear it for miles,
Hear the carnival cheering
And never let it end,
The celebration has just begun!

Georgia Phillipou (11)
St Mary's CE (VA) Primary School, Portbury

Talk About Carnival!

C ha, cha, cha
A s the people dance the day away
R ushing around, colours making people gay
N ative costumes all colours of the rainbow
I mpressive structures high and metres low
V ast amounts of food and costumes
A ll of the stereos singing samba *boom, boom*
L atin carnival is fantastically great
    Keep checking your watch, no one's to be late!

Bethany Hawker (11)
St Mary's CE (VA) Primary School, Portbury

Carnival

I can see the beginning in the distance,
I wish it would come this instant,
The sun's in the sky,
As the hats go by,
I wish I was in it,
My father's in it,
I'm trying to spot his big hat,
With him, he carries his cat,
I wish I was in it,
I want to be in it.

C arnivals are good fun
A ll over America, carnivals parade round the streets
R ingmaster hats, funny hats, lots of different hats
N o one misses out on the fun
I t's all around, people dancing
V arieties of hats have been made
A ll people join the fun of samba
L ook round the corner, the marching starts there.

Alex Phillipou (10)
St Mary's CE (VA) Primary School, Portbury

Enchanted Carnival

The costumes sway like ocean breezes
The calm, gentle spirit, peacefully eases
The magical colours blend together like fruity drink
The amazing activities make you not want to blink
The people's happiness makes the atmosphere enchanted
To the spot, you become planted
The music is like the calling of our childish souls
My heart gently starts to roll!

Polly Snell (11)
St Mary's CE (VA) Primary School, Portbury

Carnivals

Carnivals are happy,
Carnivals are fun,
You can dance all night,
Hear the music playing,
So move your feet
And dance to the beat!

The headdresses are big and colourful,
There's lots of carnival cheer,
Down the streets of Rio,
Let the celebrations begin,
So dance with a friend
And never let it end!

Amelia Landon (11)
St Mary's CE (VA) Primary School, Portbury

Anger

Anger is the colour red
Anger tastes like a juicy apple
Anger looks like a red face
Anger sounds like a loud beat
Anger feels like a big bad wolf.

Luke Jones (9)
St Michael's Junior School, Twerton

Happy

Happy is the colour of an orange dragonfly
Happy tastes like a cold ice cream
Happy looks like a red poppy
Happy sounds like lots of birds singing
Happy feels like a cat rubbing against you.

Sydney Grizzell (9)
St Michael's Junior School, Twerton

Anger

Anger is the colour red
Anger tastes like hot chocolate
Anger looks like a burning fire
Anger sounds like loud fireworks.

Alicia Magner (9)
St Michael's Junior School, Twerton

Angry

Angry is the colour black, like a spider
Angry tastes like black pudding
Angry looks like a kid being hurt
Angry sounds like a bomb going off
Angry feels like someone dying.

Thomas Smith (9)
St Michael's Junior School, Twerton

Love

Love is red like a beautiful heart
Love tastes like melting chocolate
Love looks like a beating heart
Love sounds like you've just had your first kiss
Love feels like soft silk.

Sophia Bevan (9)
St Michael's Junior School, Twerton

Angry

Angry is red like hot chilli
Angry tastes like a sour brain-licker
Angry smells like a burning hot fire
Angry feels like a very hard biscuit.

Callum Harding (9)
St Michael's Junior School, Twerton

An Eagle Poem

A little mouse is in the wood
When no one would be in the wood
As a golden eagle watches it move
He is in a hunting mood
He watches it with great sight
But when will he show his powerful might?
He swoops down towards the mouse
But it never gets towards its house.

Matteo Weeks (9)
St Michael's Junior School, Twerton

Fish

Fish come in different sizes
Shiny, gold and silver
I like to eat fish fresh from the sea
A fish cooked on the barbeque
Steaming hot with sauce on top
I like to go fishing on a boat
And catch big fish with a hook.

Syd Haskayne (10)
St Thomas More Catholic Primary School, Cheltenham

Sun

The sun shines down on the world
Sometimes making it boiling hot
Warming its cold seas
Making children want ice creams a lot
It usually comes out in the summer
Making you very hot
People do not wear jumpers
When the sun comes out!

Stephen Lumbard (8)
St Thomas More Catholic Primary School, Cheltenham

Apples On The Willow Tree

Juicy Lucy saw an apple sitting on the willow tree,
I shook the tree, the apple fell off and she blamed it all on me.
I tried to tell her I was sorry, but she wouldn't listen at all,
She grabbed my collar and shouted at me
And pushed me against the wall.
Finally, she forgave me, but we didn't have much fun,
The apple was burnt anyway, because of the warm, hot sun.
So Juicy Lucy licked a lollipop all day long!

Megan Jones (9)
St Thomas More Catholic Primary School, Cheltenham

Leaf

The leaves on a tree grow big or small,
Lots of shapes like balls,
On every leaf there are cells,
When a leaf falls down it rings a bell,
That autumn time is coming near,
Now prepare for this time of year,
So you won't be able to play out in the park,
Because it's going to be dark.

Rudi Polster (9)
St Thomas More Catholic Primary School, Cheltenham

Fish

Fish can come big or small
But they cannot shop at the mall
I caught one today
And I saw another one
That swam away.

Emily Domm (9)
St Thomas More Catholic Primary School, Cheltenham

Leaves At My Window

Leaves sway, swish and slide in the wind
They fall off branches
Every day at least ten fall
I believe that some are red
Because I watch them in bed
The wind knocks them off trees
They grow back, big and small
All different, rough and smooth
Orange in autumn and brown
Bright green in summer
Nothing in winter
Gold in spring
Lovely
Leaf.

Madaleine Chambers (8)
St Thomas More Catholic Primary School, Cheltenham

Star

Stars are bright, stars are shiny
In the sky they look so tiny

In the night they come out
To sprinkle stardust all about

A wishing star is so much fun
When all your dreams have just begun.

Phoebe Middlecote (9)
St Thomas More Catholic Primary School, Cheltenham

Star

The stars shining from up above, far, far, far away
Twinkling like a light flashing in the sky.

The star is like a gold, bright, caramel crisp
Gathered with lots of stars, like a party of stars!

Beth Garthwaite (9)
St Thomas More Catholic Primary School, Cheltenham

The Sun

The sun beams down on the world,
It's sometimes on a different part of the globe,
But now it's not out today so,
We aren't going out to play.

Charlie Mustoe (9)
St Thomas More Catholic Primary School, Cheltenham

Sun

The sun is as lovely as a sweet, warm bun
The sun makes children play and run
The sun makes you warm inside your tum
It is fun to play in the sun
The sun is sparkly, she's out today!

Poppy Wall (9)
St Thomas More Catholic Primary School, Cheltenham

The Sun

The sun is bright,
The sun is light,
Shining like a star in the sky,
The sun can burn you,
It's just like a flame,
The sun is light, bright, shiny and gold.

Kerry Davis (9)
St Thomas More Catholic Primary School, Cheltenham

Heart

My heart is red, like a flower,
It is soft, like a pillow,
It is warm, like a person,
It is lovely, like a star.

Kirsty Simons (9)
St Thomas More Catholic Primary School, Cheltenham

Sun

The sun is beating down at us today
I went out to play, but it went away
The sun is fun
Especially with a bun
It is bright and if you get burnt
You will get a fright.

Ellie Garthwaite (9)
St Thomas More Catholic Primary School, Cheltenham

The Blue Woodland

When I tiptoe through the wood,
I tiptoe on a carpet of blue,
The stalks are as delicate
As spider webs.

When you are walking
Up a hill, you get blisters,
You have a look,
By golly, they're as blue as a bluebell,
Bluebells remind me of a *ring-a-ding*.

Sam Batham (9)
Westbury-on-Severn CE Primary School, Westbury-on-Severn

Carpet Of Blue

I wandered through the forest,
The bluebells looming below my feet,
They swayed in the breeze,
From one side to another,
Millions of bluebells staring at me,
A crowd of bluebells like a giant wave,
Bluebells creating beautiful smells,
The trees providing shelter for them.

Matthew Ridler (11)
Westbury-on-Severn CE Primary School, Westbury-on-Severn

Spring Blue

Sunlight cast upon the bell,
Indigo tone I know so well.
Under hedgerows, at feet of trees,
Sheltering from the storm and breeze.
Like waves in an indigo ocean,
Swaying in a gentle motion.

                              The dew sitting on the bell,
                              Maybe ringing, you cannot tell.
                              There are silhouettes like a dancing sprite,
                              Leaping, escaping, running, might.
                              Bluebells cover from floor to floor,
                              Carpet of blue for evermore.

Crystal-white shining,
Sapphire-blue blinding, binding.
When bluebells bloom, so do you,
Left, right, in a move, wave, march,
Finding blue, violet,
Fly away, bluebell pilot.

Eleanor Burrows (10)
Westbury-on-Severn CE Primary School, Westbury-on-Severn

Sea Of Blue

Bluebells swaying in the breeze,
Like the waves from the cold sea,
Indigo, violet, lilac and blue,
In the dense woodland where the trees sleep,
Bluebells covered in dew,
As if they are about to weep.

In the distance, far, far away,
A fallen tree stayed stiff as a rock,
Bluebells growing on the top,
As if it looked like a giant purple dragon,
Shaped as an old, mouldy wagon,
As it shades the delicate white bells.

Darcey Lowe (10)
Westbury-on-Severn CE Primary School, Westbury-on-Severn

A Carpet Of Bluebells

A carpet of blue swaying in the breeze,
The flowers are right beneath the trees,
The bells are ringing,
Like a *ring-a-ding-ding*,
I stroll through the woods,
It looks like I am here for good.

They are blue, purple or violet,
There's nothing better than lilac,
They remind me of a dress,
Bluebells are nothing like a blue mess,
I try not to leave a trace,
They remind me of lots of lace.

The blue reminds me of the sea,
The bluebells are underneath the leaves,
They are as delicate as thin ice,
There are many field mice,
Its beautiful smell makes me sneeze,
They're swaying and jigging in the breeze.

Elena Morris (10)
Westbury-on-Severn CE Primary School, Westbury-on-Severn

Sea Of Blue

I was strolling through the woodlands,
When I saw a sea of bluebells,
The stems were like babies' fingers,
The heads were like ringing bells,
When the wind blew past,
The beautiful bluebells rang.

The bluebells in the green forest,
Smelt like the most beautiful perfume in the world,
They were violet, indigo and mauve,
All the purple in the rainbow.

Matthew Golledge (10)
Westbury-on-Severn CE Primary School, Westbury-on-Severn

Forest Of Blue

One spring morning, I strolled through the forest,
When I saw a carpet of bluebells,
Beneath an old oak tree,
With stems like baby fingers
And flowers like china cups,
What a beautiful sight I saw that day.

Beneath a log below a tree,
Friends of the forest,
Residents of the wood,
Come and go like sparrows,
Sleeping in the cold winter
And emerging in the spring.

I carried on my walk,
Through the woodland sea of blue,
Creeping, although not one did fall,
Swaying in the breeze like waves on the sea,
When I came to the church,
I stood in a wedding line.

Jack Mantle (10)
Westbury-on-Severn CE Primary School, Westbury-on-Severn

Blue, Blue, Bluebell

I was strolling through the woods,
One summer afternoon,
When I met with the sight of bluebells,
On the way, it was a carpet of pure blue
And indigo, as delicate as horse hair,
Have to save the bluebells,

From being knocked down
Can't leave a trace,
Help save the bluebells,
We have to save them now,
We can't just say, 'Ciao!'
We've got to save them *now!*

Joe Williams (11)
Westbury-on-Severn CE Primary School, Westbury-on-Severn

Forest Bluebells

As I tiptoed carefully through the woods
I saw in the corner of my eye, a violet wood
Made of bluebells
Sky-blue violet covers the floor
Like a carpet of different types of blues and purples

They came to meet me in my mind
I let my thoughts go wild
Of them running away from the loggers
Then my imagination bubble burst
Then I realised
I need to save them
As they're being cut down with the trees
I must leave, as now the night is nigh.

Emily Packman (11)
Westbury-on-Severn CE Primary School, Westbury-on-Severn

Bluebell Wood

I was strolling along in the woodland
And glanced at a carpet of bluebells,
It reminded me of bells ringing and tinging,
In the church, early in the morning,
The bells swaying and swinging against the wind,
Purple rainbow with indigo, violet and mauve.

Delicate stems like babies' fingers,
Sway in the breeze as precious as a spider's web,
Like silk or lace, as I tiptoed through
The forest of blue,
I just thought, what a wonderful planet we've got,
But then I saw the forest being chopped down
And we have loads of woods with bluebells in
And we should like our planet in every way.

Rebecca Smith (9)
Westbury-on-Severn CE Primary School, Westbury-on-Severn

Bluebell Wood

Bluebells dancing in the wind,
Covering the forest floor,
As the sun sets over the hill,
There is nothing I like more,
Than wandering alone through nature's beauty,
There's not one that I don't adore.

Like tiny ballerinas' skirts,
Delicate and pretty,
To know that their forests are being cut down,
Is really such a pity,
I hope that the bluebells are here for good,
The twinkling carpet in the wood.

Georgia Gibson (10)
Westbury-on-Severn CE Primary School, Westbury-on-Severn

The Forest Of Blue

The bluebells are ringing and dinging
And sway in the breeze
The colour of a violet wedding dress
The bluebells sound like church bells
As we tiptoe through the woods
All of the purple colour
Like indigo and lilac
The rainbow surrounded the Forest of Dean
A carpet of blue
My eyes were starting to shine
The stalks look like babies' fingers
And as precious as spider webs
They are blue like the sea and sky.

Tom Williams (9)
Westbury-on-Severn CE Primary School, Westbury-on-Severn

The Carpet Of Blue

A dash of wind blows through,
The bluebells are as blue as the sky,
As loud as a bell,
They're found in the lightest of forests
With a lot of sunlight
With a tiny glimpse of wonder.

The wind came crashing down,
Into the forest,
I came tiptoeing down the forest
And homes of animals and plants were gone
And the carpet of blue was all gone
And I'll remember it always.

Michael Stalker (9)
Westbury-on-Severn CE Primary School, Westbury-on-Severn

Woodland Bluebells

I see a carpet of dusty bluebells
On the woodland floor
They remind me of the sky, sea and much more
Suddenly, I saw them move, swaying in the breeze
In a shady spot, under the blossoming trees
I kept on down the path
And the carpet carried on.

As I walked on, there were other flowers
But I was more interested in the bluebells
As I got closer, I saw that it had frills on the edge
They looked really pretty
The flower as delicate as the thin layer of a glass skirt.

Sophie Jackson (9)
Westbury-on-Severn CE Primary School, Westbury-on-Severn

China Bluebells

I see violet flowers swaying
From side to side in the distance
As I wander nearer, they look prettier
The colour of their bells shows up more
So blue, they look like the sky
They glint in the sun

The stems remind me of a china tea set
I see a violet wedding dress
Shining in the sun
I hear church bells ring
Ding, ping all day long
Swaying from side to side
Reminding me of a rainbow.

Bethan Ridler (9)
Westbury-on-Severn CE Primary School, Westbury-on-Severn

Under The Sea

Under the sea live you and me
Best friends, best friends, never, never break friends
No matter what happens to you and me
We will always be best friends, don't you agree?
I don't think I'll break friends, never, ever
My best friend is kind to me and she thinks I'm clever!
My friend I can describe as she's like a part of my family
Whenever I play with her, I have good company
If I was lonely, she would come to talk to me!
'What's wrong, Holly?' she would say
'Come on, Holly! What do you want to play?'
So that's my best friend.

After you read this poem
You will probably be dying to meet her!

Holly Olinda Wyatt (9)
Widey Court Primary School, Plymouth

Tropicality

Relaxing and peaceful
A fireball gleaming
Dazzling and bright
The sun makes quite a sight!

Summer golden
Glittering cheerful
Rocky calm waves
Breaking up on the bays.

Flowing current
Sparkling and fresh
Following down beside me
To the shore ahead.

All alone . . .

Multicoloured
Buckets and spades
Leaving behind them
A deep hole today.

Caitlin Gerry (9)
Widey Court Primary School, Plymouth

The Blue Sky

The aquamarine sky,
The aquamarine sky,
Is as blue as the sea,
The indigo sky,
The indigo sky,
With clouds in the sky,
The sky blue,
The sky blue,
And the sun shining on all the land,
The navy blue sky,
The navy blue sky,
Is so blue and beautiful, our blue sky.

Chanelle Williams (9)
Widey Court Primary School, Plymouth

Fun! Fun! Fun!

It's time to push myself out of bed,
It's time to have some fun instead,
It's not the time to lay about,
It's time to laugh out loud and shout,
Let's go to Painton and see a bat,
Let's go to Crealy, somewhere like that,
There are things to see and stuff to do,
Why not spend this day with you,
Let's go outside for some fresh air,
Why not go to the summer fair,
Time to play under the sun,
Come on now, it's time for . . .
Fun!

Rebecca Palmer (11)
Widey Court Primary School, Plymouth

The Country

Butterflies landing on flowers,
Frogs leaping onto lily pads,
People walking by, on crunching gravel,
Looking down into the water,
They see fish swimming around
And the people say,
'The country is *excellent!*'

Savannah Hicks (9)
Widey Court Primary School, Plymouth

Nature

Magpies sweeping, tree to tree,
Bluebird tweeting, *tweet, tweet, tweet,*
Butterflies fluttering, *flutter.*

Laura Whitemore (8)
Widey Court Primary School, Plymouth

So Quiet

It is so quiet in an apple tree
It is so quiet just inside me

It is so quiet eating up my tea
It is so quiet just inside me

It is so quiet knowing Jack Lee
It is so quiet just inside me

It is so quiet just as he
It is so quiet just inside me.

Abigail Stoneman (9)
Widey Court Primary School, Plymouth

The Rainbow Poem

Red is like the volcano, wide
Orange is like the flame, hot
Yellow is like the sun, burning
Green is the like the trees, tall
Blue is like the water, rough
Indigo is like the sky, calm
Violet is like the violas, small
The rainbow poem is very calm
And it can all fit into the middle of my palm!

Matthew McDonald (8)
Widey Court Primary School, Plymouth

It Was So Quiet!

It was so quiet, I could hear the rain
It was so quiet, I could hear my teacher singing
It was so quiet, I could hear some girls being silly
It was so quiet, I could hear the flame burning
It was so quiet, I could hear my mum tap the cat bowls at home
It was so quiet, I could hear the class whisper.

Courtney Hackett (9)
Widey Court Primary School, Plymouth

Missing

Has anyone seen my mouse?

I opened his box for half a minute,
Just to make sure he was still in it
And while I was looking, he jumped outside!
I tried to catch him, I tried, I tried . . .
I think he's somewhere in the house,
Has anyone seen my mouse?

He must be somewhere, he must, he must . . .
I need to find him before he starts making a fuss,
He doesn't smell like a rose,
But he has a snuffly nose,
Has anyone seen my mouse?

He could be in my bedroom,
Maybe I'll look in Ted's room,
Oh, he has to be about,
He's just got out!
I think he's somewhere in the house,
Has anyone seen my mouse?

Emily Wooltorton (10)
Widey Court Primary School, Plymouth

Spider!

Spider in the bath
Spider in the bath
Doesn't it make you laugh
There's a spider in the bath!
I want to wash my hair
I just don't dare
There's a spider in the bath
I want him out of there!

Tess Lyddon (10)
Widey Court Primary School, Plymouth

Night

Night makes me feel gracious like a dolphin in the sea,
It inserts happiness into my soul,
Night is a well-meaning, sympathetic, well-mannered person
With a loving heart like a harmless little angelfish
Swimming gracefully in the ocean,
Night moves gracefully and strolls along the frosty, dark alley,
He lives on a star as if he is a king in his palace,
He wears floaty, graceful clothes,
Night has a smooth, calm face with small eyes glistening like a star
His mouth is minute and his nose is ample.

Charlotte Floyd (11)
Widey Court Primary School, Plymouth

I Had A Word

I had a word with the angels
As I sat quietly one day
I told them what you mean to me
And that you are special in every way
I asked if they would be so kind
By always being there for you
In everything you do.

Sarah Horswell (10)
Widey Court Primary School, Plymouth

The Sea

The ruby-blue sapphire water overlapping the sand
The people sparkling in the sun
With ice creams licking at the seaside
The seagulls are like a yellow diamond gliding around the sun
And the lighthouse shining like a green spotlight
Appearing around the sea.

Ashley Hutchings (9)
Widey Court Primary School, Plymouth

Is This What War Is Really Like?

As the metal monsters appear upon the horizon,
I take a deep breath, not knowing what will happen,
My heart pounds in my ear, I am so frightened,
Thud, thud, it has begun,
Is this what war is really like?

The crackling fires, orange and red,
Illuminate the night sky,
The enemy approach across a murky landscape,
Crack, crack, shells explode like an open fan,
Is this what war is really like?

We march on, so tired, so distraught,
Barely able to carry our weapons,
With only hope and love keeping us existing,
Bang, bang, gunshots fly through the air,
Could this be my day to die?

Emily Carter (11)
Widey Court Primary School, Plymouth

When I Wake Up!

Every day when I wake up
I always try to go back to sleep
I always remember that I have to get up to go to school
To learn to get a job
If we do not go to school
We will not get a job and would be very poor
But when we get a bit older
We will get a bit more money
If we did not have money, we would not have schools
But when I go it is fun, because all the teachers are nice
And so are my friends and my class
And my school is just great!

Joe Balsdon (8)
Widey Court Primary School, Plymouth

The Poppy Field

The poppy-red field
Covered in blood

Streams into the streets
The cries of sorrow heard by tomorrow

Death dawning
Bodies disintegrating
In blood-red pools of sorrow

Buildings blown up by Germans
Bombs fall everywhere

Families despair
For those for whom they care.

Holly Owens (11)
Widey Court Primary School, Plymouth

Heart Which Is Broken

The birds singing in the trees,
Outside feeling the gentle breeze,
The green grass swaying side to side,
The grasshoppers leaping with pride,
The willow tree crying tears,
But now he has no more fears,
The daffodils growing in the spring,
'It's not yet over,' says the king,
So come on heart which is broken,
Now the magic words have been spoken.

Danielle Wills (9)
Widey Court Primary School, Plymouth

Teachers

Teachers can be funny, although what they do,
They are doing it for a lot of money,
Some teachers can be tall and some teachers can be small,
Teachers can be very sporty and some teachers,
Not all the time, can be very naughty,
Some teachers are very strict, they have to be
Because us children are naughty, like Naughty Nick,
Some teachers are very brainy in our sessions
And in our class, we never listen in our lessons,
Some teachers love to talk and at lunchtimes maybe,
They might even go for a slow walk.

Jade Hawkings (9)
Widey Court Primary School, Plymouth

Bird On The Wing

It was so quiet
I could hear a bird singing so clearly
I peered out of the window
And into the sky
I saw the bird going fly, fly, fly
So now I stare at that little spot
Where that bird flew a lot
So now it's time to spread its wing
Let's hope he comes back next spring.

Hannah Ford (9)
Widey Court Primary School, Plymouth

Night

Night is a woman
She makes me feel scared
Her face is all wrinkled
With bags under her eyes
Her eyes are the colour of fire
Her mouth is as pale as a zombie
Her hair, as dirty as mud
Her clothes are made of bandages
When she moves, skin falls off her body
When she speaks, teeth fall out of her mouth
She lives in a tomb with a bat and coffin
Night scares me
Night is mad, night is sad.

Jordan Moore (11)
Widey Court Primary School, Plymouth

Catz

Cats are all shapes and sizes,
Some fat, some thin, some tall and some small,
Some black, some white and even some more,
But mine is orange, black and green
And likes to be clean,
He leaps like a frog and lands on all fours,
He tends to catch birds,
So that's my moggie, orange, black and green
As happy as can be.

Purrrrrr!

Chloe Blackmore (10)
Widey Court Primary School, Plymouth

Different Weather

There is different
Weather
Listen to this.

The sparkling sun scorches
It glistens in the
Deserts.

The power-breaking thunder
Torn and lashing
Against
The wind.

The dripping, rippling rain,
Plopping against
The roof.

The roaring, whooshing wind
Moaning.

The glittering mini golf balls
Shaped like a spiderweb
Gently float
Down.

Ryan Hateley (9)
Widey Court Primary School, Plymouth

Seasons

Howling, whooshing,
Icy snow cold,
Iced-over frozen lakes,
The snow lays so bold,
A blanket covered grass green,
Rushing so mean.

Bouncing, gazing,
Fresh dew covered grass,
Lambs timid take steps,
Across the farmer's warm grass,
Calm and gentle,
As the people settle.

Hot, sunny,
Days of fun,
Laughter and chatter,
People in the boiling sun,
Silent waves roll,
A quiet soul.

Falling, tired,
Leaves orange fall,
The trees big,
The trees tall,
Rustling small,
Is winter's call.

Sacha Mills (11)
Widey Court Primary School, Plymouth

On The Mountain

Here I am, at the foot of the mountain,
I take a quick glance at the size of it, just before I begin,
I grab my hiking gear and take my first step,
After an hour, my palms are sweaty with all my sweat,
Sweat trickles down my face, glistening in the strong sunlight,
My hands and feet protest at every effort and step in sight,
But here I see it; the snow-capped tops,
This inspires me to go faster!
I almost run up the jagged side non-stop,
The rocks become more level and even,
I can almost walk without having to cling
Onto the side of the mountain,
The ground is flat, with large boulders
And tall rocks, side by side,
I stand up tall, with my arms out wide,
The cold bitter wind biting at my face,
My hair blowing wildly behind me,
I look down, I feel strong and big, intimidating a tall oak tree,
I can see other jagged mountains
Which protrude out from the hard ground,
Although it is freezing, I feel hot with pride and happiness all around,
It is as if my warmth melts the snow
Causing it to trickle down the mountain,
My numb lips are almost burnt by the hot tea I have brought with me,
I sit until the sun goes down and take a look at the picturesque sea,
I pitch my tent and snuggle down into my warm sleeping bag,
Knowing I need a good night's sleep for the journey back.

Anna Chow (11)
Widey Court Primary School, Plymouth